Tireless

A Reporter's Life

Donna Halvorsen

Rocket Science Press
SHIPWRECKT BOOKS PUBLISHING COMPANY

IN®
DIE

Minnesota

Cover and interior design by
Shipwreckt Books

Shipwreckt Books Publishing Company
309 W. Stevens Avenue
Rushford, MN 55971

Library of Congress Control Number 2021943830
Copyright © 2021 Donna Halvorsen
All rights reserved.
Copyright © 2021 Rocket Science Press
ISBN- 978-1-7334804-9-9

To my late grandmother, Marie Johnson, and her daughter, my mother, Evelyn Hasleiet, who didn't have the chances I had, but gave me life and strength through the years. To our daughter, Darcy, the fourth generation of the Hasleiet/Johnson women, who absorbed the trials and tribulations of those who went before and used those experiences to chart her own course, who gave of her talents to all who asked and brought joy to a family who adored her.

To Jon, the love of my life for 53 years, my best friend and hero in our long, abiding partnership, through good times and bad. The father of our lovely daughter, who showed her what character looks like, and who, with joy, humor and devotion showed us both an adventurous life. Jon, who gave of himself to so many people, who lived the end of his too-short life with grace and dignity, he is my North Star still.

"You own everything that happened to you. Tell your stories. If people wanted you to write warmly about them, they should have behaved better."

—Anne Lamott

1. I'm being held by my mother Evelyn (in the middle). My brother Verdon is below Dad, Alfred. The other woman is Dad's sister, Cora; the other kids are hers. The photo was taken by Grandpa Charley in the mid-40s. I'm guessing I'm 2 years old, which would make it 1946. Charley and Mary both died the same year.

Chapter 1

hen Roy Johnson came over the clattering iron bridge into my tiny Minnesota hometown he couldn't be shocked by what he saw. Truth was, he could see only shadows. He couldn't see the church, the school, not Main Street, not the hills that framed the town, the smallness of the place.

We kids eagerly awaited his arrival, though we were a little nervous too. He was blind, and he was coming to be our English teacher. I conjured up an image of a tall, skinny man wearing a black suit and hat and carrying a briefcase, kind of like the Fuller Brush man. But the slender young man with the blond crew cut who now stood in front of our classroom wasn't in my picture at all. He looked like us. He had a ready smile, which put us kids at ease.

He came to Peterson, a Norwegian town of 318 people, because fifty other communities had turned him down flat when he sought a teaching job. Some rejections were based on school policies. Some were based on prejudice. All were based on the premise that "a blind man can't teach." How magnificently Roy was to prove them wrong.

Roy became blind while a student at St. Olaf College in Northfield, Minnesota. He went off to braille school, then began searching for a job. He was in his twenties, with a wife and young children at home. When he entered our ugly cinderblock classroom that first day he didn't seem nervous. We were the nervous ones; we didn't know quite how to treat him. But he put us at ease because he radiated confidence—confidence that, over time, made us feel more confident about ourselves. If he had any uncertainty about teaching sighted students for the first time, it didn't show. "It was a funny thing," he told me three years later. "I never had any question about how to handle it, and that's the gospel truth. I simply knew I could do it."

He had, without a doubt, the sharpest, most penetrating mind that was ever put to the task of educating Peterson's young. By educating, he didn't mean filling our minds with facts that we could give back to him on tests. He revived the lost arts of impromptu speaking and writing in the classroom, which were scary for us at first. He continually asked us, "What do you think?" at a time when most of us were not accustomed to serious thinking. He brought current events meaningfully into a classroom that was so remote from the places where history is made. All the while, he was writing his own little chapter in local history.

It helped that he was an outsider. He didn't have the time or inclination to gossip about who came from a good family and who didn't. It meant he wasn't schooled in Peterson's eccentricities, including the unspoken rule against achievement. About three hundred people were scattered over the Peterson valley when I grew up there, and I'm guessing all of them knew that Peterson had an Eleventh Commandment: "Thou shalt not be different." That was just one of the distinctive features of the little Norwegian Minnesota town that Roy entered when he crossed that iron bridge.

Chapter 2

he town of Peterson was founded in 1853 by Peter Peterson Haslerud, one of Minnesota's earliest and most enterprising Norwegian settlers. At the turn of the twentieth century, Peterson seemed poised to burst out of its little valley, with factories that made harnesses, caskets, and wagons; and it could boast of three taverns, a surgeon, a fur buyer, an embalmer, a bank, a newspaper, and a town band.

But the times passed it by. When our family moved there in 1949, it had settled down into a solemn burg of 318 people that still had the necessities: a hardware store, a general store, a restaurant, two gas stations, a butcher shop, and two Norwegian Lutheran churches. Located in a green valley with a river running alongside it, it was a pretty little place—not quite Currier and Ives, but it had a handsome stone school, a wooden bandstand, a railway station, a tiny granite town hall, and a towering feed mill.

It was a narrow valley, and when I stood in my yard the horizons were at the end of my nose, as if the world started and ended right there. The five north-south streets ended in cornfields. The three east-west streets pointed at bluffs over which the sun rose with anticipation in the morning and set with sweet relief in the evening—not so sweet when black clouds sat on the horizon on hot summer afternoons, threatening the wrath of angry skies.

There were no street signs. Everybody knew where they were and where they were going. It was heaven for young kids. It was impossible to get lost. Neighbors sent you home when they heard your mother calling. The noon whistle told you when it was time to go home to eat.

My family moved to Peterson from our backwoods homestead in Diamond Creek so that my older brother, Verdon, could go to school. The one-room school that Dad and his siblings attended had burned down. Peterson was ten miles from Diamond Creek and just four miles from Dad's job at the electric co-op in Rushford. It was still smack in the middle of Norwegian farming country.

I cried when Verdon went to school that first fall morning. I was five and had to wait another year. But it wasn't long before my brother, Wayne, was born and I was no longer my mother's sole focus, so I was free to roam. I raced a new friend to pick morning glories. I walked a half block to the school at noon to watch the kids play ball or hopscotch. Once in a while my mother sent me to Agrimson's store uptown for a pound of coffee or a spool of thread. She didn't realize that I had to pretend I was invisible to walk those few blocks—invisible because I was afraid to run into someone and have to talk to them; I couldn't hear well, and wasn't sure I could manage a conversation. My hearing deficit was intertwined with my shyness. Somehow getting the mail was easier, especially when the days grew short and dark. Just before five o'clock we'd be in the post office, a few adults and one invisible kid, waiting for the mail truck.

On torpid Saturday nights in summer, when the heat was held captive in the valley, farm families came into town to talk crops, buy staples, and socialize. "How's the corn growin' then?" one would ask. "Not bad," was the acceptable answer. We kids watched movies up against the grain elevator. I got books from the library, a musty-smelling room in the back of town hall that was open only on Saturday nights in summer.

On Memorial Day we had a ceremony at the little bandstand. I loved "In Flanders Fields," the famous World War I poem, and I yearned to read it at the ceremony, though I never got asked, thankfully. It wasn't a job for an invisible kid. As I grew older, I played in the band and watched the old soldiers valiantly try to fire rusted-out guns. I liked the valor of their efforts and the solemnity of the occasion.

On weekdays the town whistle blew at noon, alerting the men at the feed mill to shake the grain dust off their overalls and go to the cafe for dinner. The food was the comfort food I crave still: roast pork or beef, baked chicken or meatloaf, mashed potatoes, and pie, often cooked by my mother, who worked at Clarissa Johnson's, then Helen Atkinson's cafes. She was known as a great cook and the best pie-maker for miles around. She and a friend also took on big catering jobs for places like the American Legion, making forty dollars each for cooking for a hundred or more people. Once they were asked to cook a bear and a raccoon. No problem. Throw it in an enormous pot with water and lots of salt and pepper and cook it a long, long time.

2. Downtown Peterson, Minnesota, mid-1950s.

3. Mom, right, at her brother's restaurant in Rushford, with sister-in-law Lucille, mid '50s. She also worked at three cafes in Peterson over the years

Chapter 3

The church ladies didn't know I was shy and hard-of-hearing when they sent me out knocking on doors to raise money for charity, sparing themselves the unseemly task of asking for money in a town where there wasn't much of it. Once I got the hang of it I thought, "If people will give me money, maybe they'll buy something from me." I wanted money to start a stamp collection. I ordered garden seeds through the mail, never thinking how hard it would be to peddle them in the dead of winter. Then I tried Christmas cards, which went over a little better, but I concluded that sales wouldn't be my life's work.

You don't know when you're a kid that there's something wrong with you. My parents figured out when I was seven that I couldn't hear very well, and I had my adenoids and tonsils removed, the treatment in vogue at the time. It didn't work. A nurse told me afterward that I would have to "try harder" to hear. She didn't tell me how to do that, so I had to figure it out on my own. I developed a fierce concentration, taught myself to lip read, sat up front in class whenever possible. Sometimes I just tuned out. Of course, I didn't tell anyone I couldn't hear very well, not my teachers, not my classmates, no one. It was shameful. I felt like I or my parents had somehow caused this. Such was my hearing life well into my thirties, when my hearing loss was found to be moderate to severe.

I am sure it contributed to my shyness, but my workarounds enabled me to have friends and to succeed in school. And I found other amusements. In winter I did the town census in my head, starting near the bridge over the Root River, turning onto Main Street at Nels Larson's shoe shop, ending at Ernie Johnson's house on the road out of town. I visualized each house and wrote down the number of people living in it. I knew who lived where in Peterson from my door-knocking excursions, and Peterson people didn't move much back then; they didn't die very often either, and there were hardly any babies born, so this exercise of totaling up the population was kind of like counting your toes and fingers. But I didn't learn much else about the town or its people. Norwegians just weren't talkers. There's the story about the Norwegian farmer who loved his wife so much he nearly told her.

In summer I got together with my friends, Susie Benson, Pat Olson, and Beverly Johnson. As teenagers we hung out at the root beer stand just across the bridge, a pleasant addition to summers that were dull and horrendously hot. We did what teenage girls did: We giggled and gossiped and talked about boys, usually out-of-town boys, usually basketball players, who seemed exotic and were so out of reach.

The Root River was right there, but we didn't swim in it. It was dirty and hazardous, and I didn't know how to swim anyway. Fillmore County was the only one of Minnesota's eighty-seven counties that didn't have a lake, though a lake often appeared in the spring when the river overflowed and people canoed up and down Main Street.

When I was really desperate for something to do, I pruned the trees in our yard. My dad was never happy to come home from work to find me high in a tree. My mother wasn't pleased with the pile of branches I left behind. Mayor Earl Hoff kept a tidy town. He didn't like branches or junk cars or anything else lying around, so if somebody didn't pick up those branches we'd be in big trouble. It was hard to imagine what kind of trouble—criminal, civil, or moral—but no one ever got arrested in this town, where church and state were one. A raised eyebrow got the job done.

When you're a kid growing up in a small town, who's to know that the place where you live is a bit odd? Who knew that when you walked up one street and down the other nearly everybody in every house was Norwegian, and that the Lutheran church told them what they couldn't and shouldn't do. That they couldn't dance, or mow their lawns on Sunday, or have a beer after work? Or be a Democrat? Or worse, a Catholic?

As a kid would you even care? Kids don't care. They just want to be fed and set free to live their carefree lives. I didn't know what made the town the way it was until well into adulthood, when I read that many Norwegian immigrant communities were desperate to fit into their new country. Some of the early arrivals had been, shall we say, a bit rowdy. (You never saw a rowdy person in Peterson, believe me.) Norwegians were fiercely proud of their heritage, and intent on stamping out the drinking that had been a problem in their homeland. That may explain why Peterson's taverns were shut down by petition-toting women at the turn of the twentieth century. In the 1950s the American Legion bar was the only watering hole in town, though it was not allowed to have a sign out front trumpeting the vice within.

Lutheran churches in some Norwegian communities created strict moral codes that made their towns beacons of propriety: No this, no that. The Norwegian historian Odd S. Lovoll, in his book *The Promise of America*, wrote, "All Lutheran congregations, from the high-church to the low-church, were puritanical in the sense that they consistently assailed frivolity and worldly pleasures, drinking, dancing, wearing of frivolous clothes, and breaches of the Sabbath." In one small town, Lovoll pointed out, the minister even outlawed cosmetics, permanent waves, bowling, and card playing. He allowed roller skating only when kids went to a Norwegian-owned rink. "The pastor frequently became the undisputed leader in the immigrant community."

Although Peterson's deprivations weren't as bad as some, when a new minister came to town in the 1950s, he set the rules. Darn, I thought (though I would not have spoken that profane word), he's making up these rules to keep us kids from having fun. But Pastor Asp had kids, nice kids, and maybe I was wrong to make him the bad guy. He was a Norwegian pastor following a Norwegian Lutheran code when he unleashed Peterson's Twelfth Commandment: Thou shalt not dance.

4. Schoolmates Susie, Pat and Bev.

5. The old Peterson school.

Chapter 4

I didn't understand the dancing thing. People in other towns had wedding dances. Other schools had proms. And while banning dancing was one thing, inflicting your authority on individual kids was quite another. Pastor Asp told one girl who had gone to a dance in nearby Rushford, "If I hear you going to one more of those, or any dance anywhere, you will not be confirmed."

But times were changing. Television came to Peterson in the mid-1950s, throwing a wrench into extreme Lutheranism. I was mesmerized by *American Bandstand*. If this is dancing, it didn't look like sin to me, it looked like joy. Although I had to admit that the dancers' body movements might have been unsettling for Norwegian Lutheran adults, who tended not to gyrate much.

Fortunately, Peterson moms and dads didn't watch *American Bandstand*. They didn't have time to kill in the middle of the afternoon. If they had seen it just once, they might have pulled down the antenna that Stanley Agrimson had installed on the bluff, all of our TVs would have gone dark, and we would have lost the three often-fuzzy channels that made it into our valley.

American Bandstand prompted me to write a paper for a teacher who was a subscriber to the Lutheran code, asking him to explain why we couldn't dance. I argued in my paper that if we were allowed to have dances in town we wouldn't have to rely on our parents to take us to events out of town. His response was, "Don't you like your parents?" I dropped the subject.

In our sophomore year a bunch of girls decided to challenge the unwritten ban. Some of the girls had out-of-town boyfriends and actually knew how to dance. We got the approval of some of the town fathers—those who were of the non-churchy persuasion—to use the basement of town hall, and we planned the dance for a Friday night after a basketball game. We cleaned out the cobwebs, put up streamers and brought in a record player. After the game we waited for the boys, most of whom were on the basketball team. Somehow the coach, Bernie Benson, got wind of our little event (did he have the same spies as Pastor Asp?) No sooner did the boys arrive than Bernie showed up to usher them out by the scruffs of their necks. Bernie was a great coach—he coached all the sports— but he could be mercurial, and on this occasion his voice could be heard all the way to Iowa, "Get out of here, you numbskulls! If you weren't so concerned about this dance, we would have won the game!"

That was the end of attempts to dance in our town until years later, when my brother Wayne—five years my junior—and two buddies broke the ban. They were smarter than we were. They got permission to use the Legion Hall on a Saturday night (no coach to deal with that way), hired a band and charged admission. Those rebels went home with six dollars profit each. But they didn't go to church the next day. They knew the sermon would be about them—and it was, about "vipers in our midst."

§

The coach had another complaint about me, one far worse than my polemic about dancing. It was about that dashing young presidential candidate, John F. Kennedy, to whom my cousin Barb Mattson and I had taken a liking. The problem was that JFK was not only a Democrat, he was a Catholic. In our catechism training our pastor taught us about the differences in Lutheran and Catholic theologies, and the dangers of the latter. The Catholics believed in funny things like confession and purgatory. We didn't have to confess our sins to the pastor. He already knew them. And we didn't have a halfway point where we could take a deep breath, think about how hot it would be in hell (hotter than a Peterson summer?) and bargain our way out. Shucks, no. We went straight to hell. We Norwegian Lutherans had to toe the line, no second chances for us. And yes, we did toe the line, pretty much. The worst thing we could ever do, the pastor told us kids, was marry a Catholic. I knew one girl who dated a boy from the only Catholic family in town. The pastor told her, "You can't make this relationship permanent. If you do, you will not be allowed in my church."

When Barb and I put up a Kennedy banner above the lockers in school we didn't think of JFK as Lutheran or Catholic, Republican or Democrat. We thought he offered new hope for the country, along with a touch of glamour. Our views were, of course, shaped by this new, dangerous medium of television, which lacked a Norwegian Lutheran filter. We could see Camelot before our very eyes.

Our banner was gone the next morning. And after school two teachers descended upon me in the empty hallway and tried to convince me of the error of my ways. I don't remember if they said JFK would take orders from the Pope and we'd all become part of a Catholic world order that wouldn't allow us to eat *lutefisk* (yay!) and *lefse* anymore. It was something like that. This "conversation"— two adults against a kid—rattled my sensitive brain and seemed to go on forever. Maybe it was just a few minutes, but I was no match for these guys. I went home and went to bed, an icepack on my head.

Of course, Barb and I were happy when JFK won, but we kept it to ourselves.

I went to church, Sunday school, Luther League, choir practice, confirmation classes, and "release time," in which we were let out of school weekly to be instructed by the pastor in More Lutheranism (in case we'd missed something in those other venues). But I never got the hang of hating Catholics. I was, in fact, so put off by this attack on people in the name of religion that I left the Lutheran church when I left Peterson and never went back to the church (except for one time, when I got married there.)

Nothing was ever said about our banner again, or about my shameful Democratic tendencies, and I could not know then that it foreshadowed major themes in my life in the coming years. I wonder if this political fervor burbled up from some submerged Norwegian populism. My parents certainly weren't Democrats. Politics wasn't on their radar. We weren't Catholic either. We were one hundred percent Norwegian, and we tried hard not to be different.

6. My family moved to Peterson from our backwoods homestead in Diamond Creek so that my older brother, Verdon, could go to school.

7. Grandpa Charley's photo of a harvest on a nearby farm.

Chapter 5

Peterson perceived itself to be an egalitarian town, but it wasn't just a Peterson thing, it was a Norwegian thing. The principle is that we are all the same. Achievement is not a good thing. You don't want to give the impression that you are better than anyone else. This rule even has a name, which our families unwittingly brought from Norway: *janteloven*. On the good side it emphasizes equality, and forms the basis for social welfare policies in Norway that lead it to be ranked number one on the UN's Inequality-Adjusted Human Development Index, and number five on the World Happiness Report.

But on the individual level, growing up in a culture of janteloven can lead a child to internalize such notions as, "Don't think you're anything special." "Don't think anybody cares about you." "Don't think you are good at anything." In short, don't stand out.

The idea of "all being the same" had a funny effect on people. Peterson was a farming community and farmers were naturally happy when they had good crops, given the ebb and flow of agriculture and the effect it had on their families. But if a farmer goes to town and another farmer asks him, "How's your corn doin, Ole?" Ole doesn't say, "Best crop ever!" He says, "Not bad." It is a culture of, "It is what it is," and its corollary, "It could be worse."

Though I'm not sure if anyone in Peterson had heard the term *janteloven* in the 1950s, everyone knew what behavior was required of them. Although it didn't keep some from sidling up to the bar in the basement of the American Legion, drinking did make you different and, in the Empire of Lutheranism, it cast a shadow over your worth as a human being.

Janteloven is still a cultural norm in Norway and is fiercely debated. Some say it creates a nice level society. Others say it stifles economic and individual creativity. Either way, the philosophy did not translate well to a fiercely capitalist society where people fought to survive in a new land; and where some Norwegian immigrants inadvertently got rich, such as hotelier Conrad Hilton, who occupied a branch just off our family tree. It was plain, even to us Peterson kids, that some people had more money than others. Our house was just a block away from two brand new ranch houses, which certainly stood out in this 100-year-old town.

Here are some of the principles of janteloven:

Don't believe you are something; don't think you are anything special.

Don't imagine yourself better than us.

Don't believe you know more than us.

Don't laugh at us.

Don't believe you are capable.

Don't believe anyone cares about you.

In February 2018, after the Norwegians had won thirty-nine Olympic medals, a New York *Times* headline read, "As Medals Pile Up, Norway Worries, Are We Winning Too Much?" In an online comment on this story one Norwegian wrote that a positive aspect of this cultural norm is that Norway "takes better care of those on the bottom in regard to health care, support and education." But, he continued, "There are no superstars, and if one emerges, then the society around them starts to put pressure on them to come back to the pack. One can be ostracized real quick. My children experience some version of it in their school."

I hadn't figured out this strange cultural phenomenon when I was in school. But looking back, I realize that I felt it, and it shaped me and most everyone in our community. If you were valedictorian of your class as I was, or homecoming queen or king as my younger siblings Nancy and Wayne were, one would assume that you felt pretty good about yourself. But heaven forbid you should brag. You sucked up your success, buttoned up your smile, put on your crown and rode on the back of a convertible in the parade.

The truth is, my family was a little different. The differences were not the kind the Lutheran church rewarded with medals or even a smile from the minister. My parents ran a popular bar outside of town for a short while, and Dad had a country-western band, the Root River Ramblers, who practiced in our house on Friday nights. Beer may have been consumed.

But despite these radical tendencies in the family, the idea of a girl going to college was not something that ever crossed the mind of my parents, my teachers, or any of my classmates. That is, until Roy appeared in my life.

8. Confirmands with Pastor Asp, who is fourth from left. I'm last confirmand on right.

9. Grace Lutheran church in the 1950s still had its steeple.

Chapter 6

I t wasn't surprising that Peterson built a gym before it built a school to replace the old stone schoolhouse by the river. Sports were essential to the life of the town. The church was often the lifeblood of small Norwegian communities, but the school was as well, with concerts, plays, and sports, especially basketball. Norwegian Lutherans didn't ban sports for the boys—basketball was wholesome, it built character, and it gave the rest of us something to do on cold winter nights.

We were a David-and-Goliath town if ever there was one. Our school was smaller, our uniforms older, our buses colder. We had about forty-five boys in grades nine through twelve, but with one hard-working coach we fielded teams in football, basketball, baseball, and track.

What we lacked in talent we made up in tenacity. Under our kamikaze coach, Bernie Benson, we had guts if not glory and occasionally even a bit of glory. But because we were so often outmatched, we usually found ourselves on the wrong side of being different.

I loved everything about sports: the pomp and ceremony with cheerleaders and the band (I was too geeky to be chosen a cheerleader but played baritone in the band); the excitement, the chance to be part of something larger than myself—my team, my school, my town.

I went to all the football games, even though it meant standing on the hard, cold ground—we had no bleachers—and even though I didn't really understand the game. I had to go to those games in case my brothers were brutalized. Verdon was once in a coma for a week after a hard hit. Wayne was an exceptionally tough, fearless kid, even in the eighth grade, who made his own hard hits on opponents, even the big guys. Occasionally, we even beat Rushford, our nearest neighbor and much bigger rival. A Minneapolis newspaper reporter once wrote that for Rushford it was like getting beat up by the smallest kid on the block.

But basketball was the really big deal, because the farm boys, which meant most of the boys, were not needed on tractors during the basketball season in the middle of winter. I loved basketball, and I still do. I didn't miss a basketball game, at home or away, though I swear my feet are perpetually cold from those long rides on cold school buses wearing flimsy tennis shoes. I cheered for my brothers, I kept rebound charts for Bernie, I played in the band, I shredded Kleenex in the excitement of it all—my only way of participating in the games.

I died to compete—I knew I could do it, my family had athletic genes—but there wouldn't be girls basketball in Peterson and most other places for years. In the 1940s a bunch of fusty women had succeeded in banning girls basketball almost nationwide, claiming it was unladylike and harmful to girls' bodies.

Once in a while I got the key from the janitor and shot baskets in the gym. But I was part of a lost generation of girls who didn't get a chance to play basketball in school, and I felt the loss acutely.

§

With sports not an option, academics were my entrée to life. School introduced me to learning and gave me a way to live with, if not overcome, my shyness. My siblings all had virtues that enabled them to escape my nerdiness: Wayne was homecoming king and a basketball star! Nancy, homecoming queen and Girls Stater—that is, Peterson's representative to Girls State, an American Legion program that brought girls together from all over Minnesota to learn about civic engagement. Verdon was a track star who was popular—though not with teachers—for his comedic behavior in the classroom.

But I was not an athlete, not a beauty, not a comedian. What was left for me was being a good student. Though I knew the rules—don't look too smart; no showing off; help the boys when they ask for help; don't think you're anything special—I loved learning. And I loved everything else about school: putting out the school paper and being in the band.

On my own initiative I wrote patriotic essays for American Legion contests that won first place awards. The Legion also chose me as Peterson's representative to Girls State (like my sister Nancy seven years later.) For this event I got to travel to St. Paul, the state capital. When I got there I resented the rich, big city girls with their poise and nice clothes, but I learned lasting lessons about government and politics. It was an early introduction to interests that would blossom in my twenties, when I would become a leader in Democratic politics in Grand Rapids, Michigan.

But in a world of "don't be different," in a culture that placed no value on academic achievement, I never had a sense of where my successes could lead. One teacher at Peterson spent his algebra class extolling the virtues of families—his, and the ones we would soon fit into. Boys would be farmers. Girls would be farmers' wives. At the end of the year, we were on page fifty-seven of a two-hundred-page textbook; we didn't know much algebra, but we had a good grounding in what our culture expected of us.

A teacher told one classmate not to waste teachers' time by taking chemistry or physics or geometry "because you're going to get married and have kids anyway." Decades later this friend told me, "You don't come out of that feeling you're worth a whole lot." It took her a while, but when she was forty-three years old she went to college and became a teacher and advocate for the blind.

I wasn't good at algebra or geometry or the sciences, but I worked hard at them and got grades that were good enough—combined with As in English and other subjects—for me to become valedictorian of my class of fifteen. On the day of graduation the girl with lofty ambitions—but no certainty in her future—was scared stiff when she walked onto that stage. The cinder block gym was sweltering hot and it was packed with more people than lived in Peterson. It was 1962, and the U.S. had put a man in space just a few weeks earlier and was locked in the "space race" with the Russians. In my speech I said that if the U.S. could send an astronaut into space, we could do anything, including routing the Russians. But I'm not sure many heard what I said, terrified as I was. In the end, being first didn't do much for me. The next day I was the same person I had been the day before my big speech. My glory, such as it was, faded quickly.

In a paper I wrote for class the previous fall I said that English was my best subject and if I did go to college—highly unlikely—I hoped to major in journalism, but was considering a second major in speech. That combination might open up the fields of teaching, speech therapy (in recognition of my lisp?) and journalism. But "a remote possibility" would be something involving the United Nations: "As crucial as the world situation is today, more people are needed to further the cause of democracy." I had aspirations, but they were pipe dreams.

Chapter 7

We kids were blank slates when we entered Roy's classroom in our senior year. As a teacher Roy was tough and uncompromising. He would challenge, he would prod, but he would never coddle.

He later said that he wasn't "quite tough enough" that first year, that "I was too worried about being accepted, trying to be too much of a good guy."

But it was hard for his students to believe he could have been much tougher. In late October, after spending night after night rehearsing a class play he was determined would be successful—yes, a blind man directing a class play; that's how determined he was!—Roy scheduled a rehearsal on Halloween. "Be there or else," he said.

Though Roy, a newcomer, didn't know it, for us Peterson kids Halloween was our only night of aimless frivolity in the whole year. Call it Lutheran repression unmasked. We did silly things, like dragging the feed mill bins into the street and running off into the cornfields. The church stayed clear of our aberrant behavior. The non-churchy men in town deputized themselves to rein us in, though in fact they never caught us, and I don't know what they would have done with us if they did. Peterson didn't have a jail or, as far as I knew, even a set of handcuffs. Having worked so hard for so many nights on the play, we weren't going to miss out on our one night of fun. Only two of us showed up at Roy's rehearsal, and I wasn't one of them.

When we returned to school the next day Roy and the other teachers were furious. In our English class Roy said he had no choice but to keep teaching us, but he wanted nothing to do with us outside of class. I was editor of the school paper and he was the adviser. I quietly approached him after class and asked, "How are we going to put out the paper?"

"That's your problem," he said.

Though he kept his distance for a while, in the end, Roy couldn't be the teacher he wanted to be under those conditions, so he let himself back into our lives. This was a gesture that told us who he was: a teacher first, and he took that role very seriously.

As I entered that last year of high school, I didn't know what would become of me. Even though I had proven myself a good student, I was offered no guidance about my future. No one mentioned college, which wasn't on the radar for kids in a Norwegian farming community that frowned on achievement. But during that senior year, as Roy got to know me, he insisted that I had to go to college. Roy told me I could be anything I wanted to be. Ya, sure, you betcha! I had no money nor any way of getting any. I didn't think about applying for a scholarship, nor did I know where or how to get one. Who would give a scholarship to a kid who was first in a class of fifteen anyway? My dream of becoming a journalist floated out there in the ozone alongside asteroids and flying pigs, but Roy had a fierce belief in me.

§

And there was one other brilliant man who had awakened in me a hunger to experience more of the world, who pushed me to think of college as necessary—if not necessarily possible—and that man was the Reverend Martin Luther King Jr.

As my friend Susie Benson and I, and a bus full of Lutheran kids from Minnesota, rolled through the South in the summer of 1961 to a Lutheran youth convention in Miami Beach, we were excited to say the least. Our departure from Peterson had been delayed for nearly an hour while I had a doctor lance a boil on my nose, a problem my uncle noticed at the last minute. With my nose bandaged, we set off, driving twelve hours straight through to Nashville.

Most if not all of us had never been out of Minnesota, and what a treat it was to arrive in Nashville! It was a lively, colorful southern city that certainly was exotic to us. None of our prairie towns had this kind of élan. We slept in an air-conditioned motel, a first for most of us, and we ate grits with our eggs for breakfast.

But the joy of Nashville was, of course, going to the Grand Ole Opry at Ryman Auditorium, where I would hear the music I heard in my living room as a little girl. Many of my favorite performers were there—the ones I had heard on the radio, and whose songs my father's band, the Root River Ramblers, had played: Patsy Cline, Jim Reeves, Roy Acuff, Loretta Lynn, Don Gibson, the Louvin Brothers, and the Carter Family.

My all-time favorite country performer, Hank Williams, died eight years earlier. I wish I had seen him in 1949 when, at the age of twenty-five, he received six standing ovations in his debut performance at the Ryman. He was an instant star, so beloved that my dad cried when he died in 1953 at age twenty-nine.

The Ryman Auditorium, which began as a revivalist tabernacle in 1892, is now a National Historic Landmark for its role in popularizing country music. It also has a plaque out front citing it as the birthplace of bluegrass music, a variation of country. In this beautiful historic structure, the music went on until midnight. I left in a glow. With the Grand Ole Opry behind me and with Reverend Martin Luther King Jr. waiting in the wings, this would be a very special trip.

The bus jogged east to Savannah, where we all got out of the bus and ran up and down the streets looking at the antebellum mansions and beautiful parklike squares. Then we hugged the coast as we headed south to Miami Beach, where we would make history. This was the first ever national Lutheran youth convention, and the most important civil rights leader of our time would be there to speak to us.

We knew these were tumultuous times. On television we had watched Freedom Riders being beaten in Alabama as they challenged segregation. But we never could have imagined that the keynote speaker at our convention would be Dr. King. His seemingly radical views were threatening to many, and some Lutherans had tried to scuttle his appearance, reasoning that it wasn't a good idea to give this man a platform to influence impressionable kids. Reverend King had actually pulled out, but a couple of tenacious Lutheran ministers lured him back.

Martin Luther King Jr. couldn't do much back then without making news, and he chose to make news at our convention by saying that the church, the generic church, was the most segregated institution in America. It was quite a spectacle, this charismatic black man speaking to 14,000 overwhelmingly white Lutheran teenagers. His eloquence took my breath away and made tears fall. I knew I was in the presence of greatness. But I had to compose myself because I was intent on taking down his entire speech in shorthand. Once back home I transcribed the speech into a spiral notebook that I still have. One sentence always jumps out at me: "Do what you will to us, and we will still love you."

But more than the message of "love thy neighbor," which I had learned in Sunday school, I was impressed by King's exhortation not to allow yourself to become adjusted to the wrongs of the world. "Everybody wants to live a well-adjusted life," he said. "I don't intend to adjust myself to segregation and all that goes with it. It is not violence or nonviolence; it is nonviolence or nonexistence. The preservation of our society lies to the maladjusted."

The idea that we didn't all have to be the same, that it may in fact be good to be different, to rebel against society's wrongs, and even against society's expectations of us as individuals, was a stunning and powerful one for a sixteen-year-old girl from a small town in Minnesota.

Of course we all know that Martin Luther King died too young, at age thirty-nine, but in my many moves over the years his words have traveled with me. That trip to Miami Beach gave me a view of the world outside my sheltered life, and a perspective on justice that awakened my conscience.

As for my other mentor, the other great man in my young life, Roy Johnson, he too died too young, at age thirty-four, from complications of diabetes. He left his wife Shirley and his young children behind. Shirley contributed so much to Roy's success. She must have been exhausted most of the time as she translated his books into braille, helped him grade papers, and tended to the many needs of their young family. I have kept in touch with her through the years.

After our class graduated, Roy became a friend to many of us. He laughed with us, talked politics with us, inquired about our personal and academic lives and asked us to visit his classroom to talk to his classes. I had not seen Roy in several years when he died, but I knew I would miss him tremendously. My sadness was not just in losing a mentor and friend, but also in knowing that so many young people would not have the experience I had. I thought they would be better people for having known him. Roy would not want to be made more in death than he was in life, but he was so much in life. He was the personification of Henry Adams' statement, "A teacher affects eternity; he can never tell where his influence stops."

If there was a single overarching conclusion of my young life, far more important than Peterson's eccentricities, it was that Roy was a gift to me, and so was Martin Luther King. It wouldn't seem that these two men had much in common, but both were enormously talented, driven men who pushed people toward what was right.

Both appealed to the best in me. Both seared my soul for life. Both gave me the courage to go to college, and finally to become a journalist. In my last years of high school, I didn't know what would become of me. Then along came these two powerful mentors. With their inspiration, I knew that I had to go to college.

Roy wanted me to go to his alma mater, St. Olaf College. But I didn't have the money for tuition, or the plaid wool skirts and cashmere sweaters I saw girls wearing in the college's brochures.

I ended up at Winona State College, only thirty miles from home. I could get one of the National Defense Student Loans that the feds were handing out like candy, no questions asked. An $800 loan paid all my expenses that first year, and I had ten years to pay it back.

My mother, who had quit school in the seventh grade to look after her mother, liked having me in Winona because I could come home on weekends. She even got me a job at a local restaurant that summer (I was a very bad waitress) so I could have some spending money.

Though I was nervous when I started at Winona State, I quickly realized that it was not going to challenge me. I got mostly As and found myself bored silly in most of my classes. I had broken the restraints of the low expectations of Peterson, but I knew that I had not yet found what I was looking for. I considered my options, and discussed it with Roy, and set my sights on the next big challenge, a decision that would set the direction for the rest of my life.

10. A great man in my young life, my teacher, Roy Johnson, was blind. He died too young at thirty-four years, from complications of diabetes.

Chapter 8

I stand in the center of the University of Minnesota's immense campus with two suitcases in hand. It is the first day of classes, and I have no place to live.

I can't go back home. I had the audacity to go off to college with $200 in my pocket, and I could not endure the snickering of the old guys who sit outside Helen's Cafe and would tell everybody who passes by, "Did you hear that ..."

The University of Minnesota, which everyone calls "the U," occupies 1,200 acres and hosts 40,000 students. I don't know any of them, and I don't know where anything is. I hope I can work this out and find a place to live so that I can navigate my new school and make some new friends. I leave my suitcases at the job service office and go off to my classes.

How did this happen? Finally I am starting my real college career and how does it begin: homeless in Minneapolis! I spent the summer with a job as a nanny outside Chicago. I sent my weekly earnings of twenty-five dollars home to my mother. Near the end of the summer I arranged by phone to become a housekeeper for a woman and her two grown daughters in a St. Paul suburb. The plan was that I would ride to school each day with one of the daughters. I arrived early, with time to settle in, and on the weekend before classes began, while dusting a bookshelf, I saw a police mug shot of one of the daughters, the daughter whose bedroom I was sharing. A police mug shot! What could she have done? I could have asked, but I didn't. I just panicked, quickly packed my bags and bolted. Looking back I can say that I definitely should have asked. What I eventually found out is that the young woman had been a Freedom Rider, challenging the segregation of interstate buses in the South in the 1960s. That is why she had been arrested, and no doubt why her mug shot was proudly displayed on a bookshelf.

After my classes I picked up my suitcases at the job service and asked if they had any live-in jobs. In a stroke of immense good fortune, they had a job as a nanny for a couple who lived just across University Avenue, across the street from campus. I walked to the house and stashed my suitcases around the corner of the porch, not wanting to look as desperate as I was. The door opened, and there stood Ellen Herdman—tall and willowy, her reddish hair piled on her head, a radiant smile on her face. I quickly realized why she needed help. She and her husband Roger, who was doing his medical internship at the U, had four girls aged five and under. We looked at each other, she invited me in, we talked a little, and Ellen and I became a done deal. The Herdmans are friends still, more than fifty years later.

Once I emerged from crisis mode and settled in, I realized that a wonderful thing had happened. Instead of living in a far-flung suburb of St. Paul with no transportation, I was just a few blocks walk from Murphy Hall, home of the Journalism School.

I felt immense relief when Roger and Ellen took me in. I had escaped failure, for now anyway. I had a place to live, and a job, although unpaid. Now the question was, can I survive academically at the University of Minnesota, the state's flagship public institution of higher learning. When I decided to make the transfer there were three appealing things about the U: it was cheap, everybody who applied got in, and you didn't need nice clothes. Best of all, it had a journalism school, the focus of my delusional ambitions.

But I couldn't get into a journalism class my first quarter, so I took a non-journalism writing class. Turned out it wasn't really a writing class at all but a class about politics. The instructor was a wide, galumphing woman, draped in black, who strode into the classroom with an aura of contempt. One day she gave us a choice of three topics to write a paper on in class—all political. I was clueless and just picked one, about the difference between a liberal and a conservative. These were the 1960s, mind you, and even an eighteen-year-old was supposed to know stuff. The next day she read my paper in class, introducing it as "the worst thing she'd ever read." I was stunned by her nastiness and embarrassed at being singled out.

After class I sat down outside for a while and told myself, "Hey, little, small town girl with big ambitions, you should have seen this coming. Maybe striving isn't a good thing after all. Maybe you've reached above your station. Maybe you should go home and do what your mother wanted you to do: become a secretary." I could do that. I was a whiz at typing and shorthand.

I went back to talk to Ellen. Her kindness and my stoicism kept me from going over the edge. She was appalled at the instructor's nastiness and said she should have taken me aside instead of shaming me in front of the class. Ellen assured me that it was just a tiny bump in the road, and the days ahead would be better. I put my blinders back on and plodded ahead.

The next quarter things started getting better. I began taking journalism classes, and I met my mentor, Professor George Hage. I learned my craft in George's classes, and shortly after meeting him found myself working on the student newspaper, the Minnesota *Daily*. Professor Hage gave me no choice: "You need to work for the *Daily*," he said. "I'm taking you down there."

The city editor looked at me skeptically and gave me a news release to rewrite. When I handed my copy to her she said, "Get the gobbledygook out of that lead." It meant I'd messed up, but she took me on anyway. The presence of George Hage, the prince charming of the J School, couldn't have hurt. So just like that, I was working for a newspaper. And they were going to pay me! Only much later did I learn that the Minnesota *Daily* was the largest college newspaper in the world.

I began working for the *Daily*, and soon I actually had a beat: I was the religion reporter. This meant going around to the student religious houses gathering information and writing stories about their activities. Not exactly Pulitzer-caliber journalism, but when I realized that I was getting paid fifteen cents an inch instead the minimum ten cents, tiny Norwegian fireworks went off in my head—I was valued, I was succeeding. I doused those fireworks quickly, of course. Professor Hage also gave me good grades on my class work. Maybe, I thought, I might become a journalist after all.

It was an immense relief to be paid by the *Daily*. I kept a tight grip on my spending as my summer earnings dwindled. Tuition was fifty-eight dollars the first quarter, but one hundred five the second. I bought second-hand books, then sold them back to the bookstore when the classes were over. I didn't buy clothes; even the kids with money looked rumpled.

The *Daily* was a strange and crazy place, a big room filled with old desks and manual typewriters, anchored by an old-fashioned U-shaped wooden copy desk, just like in the movies. It was located on the ground floor of Murphy Hall, so when we needed to go to the printing press downtown, we just climbed out the windows.

Some of us actually worked there and depended on the Daily for income. Others just hung out, and I couldn't tell if they ever went to classes; they were just happy to have a place where their eccentricities were accepted—though not necessarily by me; I harbored a bias against snitty city kids who didn't have to pay for their education. Once, at a *Daily* party, someone stole two weeks of my pay, leaving me dead broke. It was the only time I had to ask my parents for money. My mother was upset, "Why would somebody steal money from you when you work so hard for it?" she asked. But she didn't hesitate to give me money to tide me over.

It didn't matter what I wore, but I owned only one pair of slacks, so I had to wear what I had, skirts and dresses, which meant my knees froze when heart-stopping winds swept off the Mississippi River. My extreme frugality found room for one extravagance: I bought myself a pair of knee-high boots. They made me feel fashionable, up to my knees at least.

§

My experience at the *Daily* enabled me to line up a summer job at a small town newspaper in Minnesota. But at the last minute the editor suddenly gave the job to someone else. I had to scramble and ended up finding a job as a maid for a wealthy suburban Minneapolis family. On the first day the wife sent me to the basement to get a uniform. The basement was cluttered with old furniture and boxes, and an old couch where I was expected to sleep. There I found uniforms of all sizes, which should have been a clue—they had had many maids before me.

The wife and two daughters of the family were nice enough, but the husband was a terror. In my young life I had known silence, but I had never I had never been yelled at. I felt that I had to put up with his tirades—without my twenty-five dollars weekly pay I couldn't stay in school. My failure to quit came with a price: my hands shook, and my hair was falling out.

Rescue came near the end of the summer when I got a call from Professor Cam Sim, telling me that the J School had a job for me if I was interested. Out of my summer misery came something extraordinary. The job was to work with two organizations, run by Skip and Kathy Leabo, that supported high school and college newspapers. Skip became a mentor and, with Kathy, made it possible for me to survive financially.

Their office was just down the hall from the *Daily*, and when I came to work Skip would be standing at the front desk with a copy of the *Daily*, ready to critique the story I had written in the paper that day. Some of the women in the office asked me, "Why do you put up with that?" I answered, "Because I'm learning." Skip was my drill sergeant, but he also was a kind and decent man and an important mentor. With Skip and Kathy I found more lifelong friends.

One of my duties was to write a national college news summary, which required going through huge mail bags of college newspapers. I would be wrestling with those bags on weekends when another journalism student, a young man named Jon, would pop into the *Daily* office and say, "I knew you'd be here."

It was Jon Halvorsen, a brown-eyed handsome man who commuted from his parents' home in south Minneapolis. When I saw him walk into the *Daily* newsroom that first day I was astounded by how good looking he was. "Nah," I said to myself, "too classy for me. He wears Gant shirts." That day I went back to my work, but he sought me out. He would leave me notes on the *Daily* bulletin board: "Are you free at 10:30 to go get the rest of our books? I hope so. By the way, you're cute." Once we connected we were drawn to each other in our shyness.

The *Daily* newsroom became my home away from home and was a welcoming place for me. I had graduated from brief stories on the religion beat to major stories, including those on university governance. Once when a vice president wouldn't return my calls I went to hear a speech he was giving and asked him my questions there. At a subsequent meeting he complimented me on my persistence.

By my senior year I was the copy desk chief, sitting at the big U-shaped desk with my own crew, daily editing the work of young student reporters. The geeky girl from Peterson was starting to feel comfortable in her own skin. I couldn't possibly feel geeky with Jon in my orbit. He even thought I was cute—imagine that!

In my senior year I unexpectedly received an invitation to the U's honors ceremony. To my surprise I was one of twenty students called to the stage to receive the North Star Award, the highest student achievement award available to the U's 40,000 students. I didn't know why, but it must have been in recognition of the reporting I had done for the *Daily*.

What would I have done without the Minnesota *Daily*? A few years later, on my first job, in Albany, New York, some of the old-timers snickered that they didn't have to go to journalism school to learn how to be reporters. But for me, the J School and the *Daily* were essential. They gave me training, reporting experience, much-needed income, and the joy of fitting in.

As graduation neared, one day I was walking down the corridor in Murphy Hall when I heard Professor Ed Emery's voice calling me. I turned around to hear him ask, "Are you in Phi Beta Kappa?" I said I wasn't. "Well, you should be," he said. "I'll take care of it." And so he did. A kind gesture by another of the J School professors who had given me so much during my years at the U.

On Cap and Gown Day I walked to the ceremony with Buzz Menold, a *Daily* staffer and good friend. Unbeknownst to us, a *Daily* photographer snapped our photo from behind. The next day it was on the paper's front page—a graphic representation of that moment in my life, walking away from the years of education and professional training, heading forward into the unknown future.

I wasn't really a well-rounded person when I graduated from the U. I hadn't taken the university's great courses taught by world-class thinkers. But I had learned my trade. I had a degree in journalism. My pipe dream of becoming a reporter felt like it was within reach.

During that senior year I lived with Ava Woolliscroft Betz, whose wicked sense of humor still makes me laugh to this day. In our first place, five people lived in a one-bedroom apartment. By the time graduation rolled around we were ensconced in a decrepit Dinkytown hotel where the smells of Chinese cooking woke us daily, and the foyer smelled like someone had died there.

That's where we were living when my friends and family arrived from Peterson to attend my graduation. No one said anything about my surroundings—after all, they were Norwegians. My parents didn't show any excitement at my success—excitement just wasn't in their DNA—but I knew that they were proud of me.

I didn't ask for my parents' advice or approval when I made the big decision to transfer to the U. I talked only to Roy. This was not an honorable thing for me to do, but I felt I was on such shaky ground with this venture, and I didn't want anyone to talk me out of it. Actually, I don't think Mom and Dad would have done that anyway. Although they never had the chance to even go to high school, they were smart, resourceful people. I knew that they were proud that I graduated first in my Peterson class. When I told them that I was leaving nearby Winona State and moving to Minneapolis they were surprised, but not judgmental. They didn't ask, "How far do you think $200 will go? Where will you live?" Such is the acceptance of stoic Norwegian parents, the parents who gave me the Norwegian immigrant genes and the work ethic that kept me going.

As we gathered for a party after the graduation ceremony a friend came over to give me a sugar and creamer set as a gift. She smiled slyly and nodded toward Jon, who was in a conversation across the room. "You're going to marry that guy," she said.

11. Donna at the U. On Cap and Gown Day I walked to the ceremony with Buzz Menold, a *Daily* staffer and good friend. Unbeknownst to us, a *Daily* photographer snapped our photo from behind. The next day it was on the paper's front page.

Chapter 9

I was sure I'd get a job. With all the awards I'd won and the encouragement I'd received, I knew I was a strong candidate. But as graduation neared, my future didn't look so great. In the spring, when newspapers made recruiting trips to the J School, no one was interested in me. One entire newspaper chain wasn't even interviewing women. The Chicago *Tribune* gave me a perfunctory interview despite my scholastic record.

Though it was a shock to me at first, eventually I got the message: Why would we hire a girl? She would just get married and have babies, and we'd have to let her go. Around this time the Minneapolis *Tribune* fired a female journalist on the day her child was born.

These 1960s-style rules for women suddenly became up front and personal for me. Shortly after graduating, I discovered that I was pregnant, the surprising result of a solitary rendezvous at a friend's cottage.

I went into hiding and yes, I thought it was necessary. Being unmarried and pregnant in the 1960s broke all of society's rules. Girls like me were sent off to "unwed mothers' homes" to give birth, and their babies often were given away to "good homes." Nothing could have been more loathsome to me.

Jon didn't tell his parents. I didn't tell mine. I knew that I could have spent my pregnancy at home. My parents wouldn't be angry. But I just couldn't face the shame of Peterson. Though the shame I felt at hiding this from my family was worse.

I moved in with the Herdmans. If I was going to be banished from good society, where better to spend my exile? Roger was a doctor, Ellen a nurse. I appeared in the kitchen at 5:00 p.m. to talk to Ellen while she cooked. She was of sturdy Vermont stock but had no Yankee reserve. Rather, she had a vibrancy that lifted me out of my funk. Daily, she reminded me by her very presence that life wouldn't always be as difficult as it seemed right then.

Except for regular counseling sessions at Lutheran Social Services, I rarely left the house. The counselor there was very brusque, very Norwegian Lutheran. When I told her that I trusted Jon and we were planning to get married, she responded, "How do you know he won't do this to another girl and leave you behind?" My response was, "He wouldn't. I know he wouldn't."

In the fall I started graduate school but quit when I began to show. I didn't tell my parents I had quit. I wrote letters to them, so they had my address, and they wrote to me. One day Dad drove up to see me without letting me know he was coming, but when he arrived, I wasn't there. I think he sensed something was wrong and wanted to make sure I was okay. It must have been a horror for him to drive two hours to "the Cities," even worse to drive in Minneapolis traffic and find Ellen's house, and sad to return home without seeing me. When I found out about this, years later, I was heartbroken. I am saddened still by my betrayal of his caring soul. But then I think: On seeing Ellen's radiant face, he must have realized I was okay. I was in good hands.

Occasionally I treated myself to coffee and pie at a nearby restaurant. The Herdmans had moved away from campus by then, so I didn't worry about running into someone I knew. But one day I noticed a car whose driver looked like the superintendent of Peterson High School. What would he be doing here? The car was moving slowly; I thought he must have recognized me. I ran home in my awkward, big-bellied body and called the school; I hung up with relief when they said they would put him on the line. I didn't go out for pie anymore.

I was grateful to have support during my pregnancy. Jon visited regularly. Ellen whisked away my shame. Skip kept me working on his projects; his smiling face cheered me when he delivered work for me to do.

Then one March morning my water broke. Ellen drove me to a Lutheran hospital where Jon met us and stayed with me until ten that night, just before my difficult labor began. Because we weren't married, he wasn't allowed in the delivery room. Ellen had four little girls to look after so she couldn't be with me. My best friend Ava was on my case about getting pregnant and exclaimed that she would never put herself through the barbaric ritual of childbirth! (She would have children.) When a nurse asked if I wanted to call someone, I said no. The nurse was love personified. She was at my side the whole time.

This puritanical hospital wasn't nice to me, but after all I was a miscreant, not entitled to niceties. Jon and Ava came to offer support to me before my labor began, but the hospital kicked them out. My Hungarian doctor didn't believe in blood transfusions, even in an extremely difficult delivery. That meant I had to stay in the hospital for five days, where I couldn't even get out of bed on my own, and it would take weeks for me to regain my strength. But hard as it was, it was all worth it when Darcy Ellen arrived, the adorable girl who would be Jon's and my only child. I was her mother, Jon was her father and we would be a family, puritanical society be damned.

Sadly, the hospital wouldn't let me hold Darcy, a trauma I relived decades later when I watched "Call the Midwife," and saw baby after baby placed in a mother's arms.

This was not news Jon wanted to deliver to his parents, but he did it, bravely. His mother, Ellen, had a close and loving relationship with her only son. She was upset that she didn't know anything about this. His father, Ted, once it sank in, had only three words to say, "I'm a grandfather!" Ted and Ellen would be wonderful grandparents.

When I called to say I was coming home, Mom knew instantly what had happened. She knew because she had given birth to a child before she and Dad got married. In fact, she had been cursed for it by some members of Dad's family. Did Dad's siblings forget that their own mother, Mary Hasleiet, was pregnant with her first child before she married their father Charley? Did they forget that their parents didn't get married in a church, but, disgracefully, in the Diamond Creek house in the dead of winter? Were they not capable of a little bit of compassion, even after seeing the four fine children that Mom raised? I was, and still am, fond of many members of Dad's family, but there were a couple who would never darken my threshold.

Mom approached my situation with her usual taciturnity and turned her attention to helping me prepare for my wedding. It wasn't my first choice for the ceremony, but we decided to hold it at Grace Lutheran Church in Peterson, so my Grandma Marie Johnson, Mom's mother, my only living grandparent, could be there. She lived in a little pink house a few blocks from the church. A tiny white-haired lady who wrote poetry and read the Bible, she had raised eight children on a farm and had two dozen grandchildren. Still, I was special to her, and she to me. She wrote to me while I was at the university, "You are one of the few. The Lord is with you giving you patience and strength besides your own intelligence in all your way, letting the world go by with all temptations. You will win in a big way, to prove what one can do." I failed the temptations part but she was on my side anyway.

Before we could get married in the Lutheran church, we had to acknowledge our sin in an audience with Pastor Asp. Not a smile nor words of encouragement followed his ministerial lashes. Autocratic Lutheran pastors—or at least this one—lacked a basic sense of humanity. I had followed his cardinal rule by not marrying a Catholic, but I didn't get any credit for bringing home a nice Norwegian lad who had been an altar boy at the largest Lutheran church in North America.

Jon had not yet graduated, and he had just added a wife and baby to his college studies. His parents may not have wanted this life for him at age twenty-one, but they helped out and found the beautiful child to be worth it all. We lived with Jon's parents in Minneapolis for a few months while Jon continued with school. I'd done a fair amount of babysitting, but I knew nothing about caring for a baby. Jon's mom, Ellen, showed me everything. We had embarrassed her, but she adored Darcy. She and Ted were wonderful to me their entire lives—they were the best of humankind. We had given them their first grandchild, and every time we visited them after they moved to Arizona, Darcy Ellen glowed under their attention.

My parents, Alfred and Evelyn Hasleiet, were happy to have their first grandchild, too. They also were happy to have a son-in-law from a good family and a daughter who, even after marriage, had a Norwegian last name.

The marriage consecrated that day lasted 53 years. I lost my "good girl" standing in town, but I didn't give a damn. Neither did my parents. When we returned to Peterson for visits over the years, people treated us kindly. Of course, they would. They didn't give a damn either.

12. Jon had not yet graduated, and he had just added a wife and baby to his college studies. His parents may not have wanted this life for him at age twenty-one, but they helped out and found the beautiful child to be worth it all.

13. Jon's Dad Ted, me, Jon's Mom Ellen, and Jon. We lived with Jon's parents in Minneapolis for a few months while Jon continued with school. I'd done a fair amount of babysitting, but I knew nothing about caring for a baby. Jon's mom, Ellen, showed me everything. We had embarrassed her, but she adored Darcy. She and Ted were wonderful to me their entire lives—they were the best of humankind.

14. Dad, me, Mom and Jon. Mom approached my situation with her usual taciturnity and turned her attention to helping me prepare for my wedding. It wasn't my first choice for the ceremony, but we decided to hold it at Grace Lutheran Church in Peterson, so my Grandma Marie Johnson, Mom's mother, my only living grandparent, could be there.

Chapter 10

U nlike me, Jon had five job offers after he graduated. Unlike motherhood, fatherhood did not seem to be a problem for newspapers looking for good reporters. We chose the Grand Rapids *Press*, the daily newspaper in the small, conservative city of Grand Rapids, Michigan.

I hoped to get a job there too, but they said, "Sorry, we have a nepotism policy." That meant that spouses of employees could not be hired. I was one of seven journalist spouses—only one a man—on the outside looking in. It was small consolation, but at every Christmas party the managing editor apologized for not being able to hire me.

It was a great place to work if you were a guy. In the winter the paper rented a gym so they could play basketball. In the summer, it paid for them to enter a softball league. There were five male reporters in their twenties, a smoldering cauldron of testosterone. At parties they sat around drinking beer, griping about their bosses and about the newspaper. One of Jon's colleagues, another graduate of the Minnesota J School, complained that the paper even accepted copy from "any old housewife." I knew he was talking about me— I had written a couple of freelance pieces—but I didn't say anything then. When I told George Hage, my J School mentor, about this guy and his comment George said, "You can write rings around him." But at the time I didn't stand up for myself, because I would have stood alone. Boys were boys well into adulthood back then. We "girls" shrugged off their excesses.

Meanwhile, the paper hired a man who walked in off the street and told them that his only experience was writing letters. "Amazing!" I thought. What a stunning breach of managerial competence and common sense. That is when it dawned on me how bad it was to be a woman in the 1960s. You bust your butt to work your way through one of the best journalism schools in the country, you graduate *magna cum laude* and Phi Beta Kappa, only to have your dreams thrown back in your face. I realized then that I might never get a newspaper job. Everything seemed to be saying: Go home and be a wife and mother. We don't want you, not now, maybe never. I was shocked to discover that the road ahead would be even rougher than the one I had already traveled. My life's course, it seemed, would be set by the culture, not by my merits.

I settled in to being a wife and the mother of a delightful little girl as we made our way in a strange—very strange—Dutch city. For Darcy and me there were playgrounds, library visits, donut excursions, friendships with other kids, and welcome visits from our far-away Minnesota families. Darcy was a gregarious little girl and she adjusted more quickly than I did, but we worked at it together. I had time to read and think.

In 1969, a year after we arrived, the women's movement hit me in the form of an article in *Mademoiselle* by Ellen Willis called, "Whatever Happened to Women? Nothing—That's the Trouble." "Male supremacy has existed for so long that it has come to seem an unalterable absolute," Willis wrote. But sexism, like racism, is "incompatible with human dignity."

Her words hit me like a great truth. I came from a Midwestern immigrant farm tradition in which women hoisted bales of hay alongside men, but also baked a dozen loaves of bread and fed a dozen farm hands daily at harvest time. The women I saw growing up seemed possessed of boundless energy. I didn't stop to think that they might also be exhausted.

My mother worked both inside and outside the home. She had never heard of equal rights. She didn't even expect thanks for her selflessness. She was not the eldest daughter, but she quit school in the seventh grade to look after her widowed mother, who was exhausted from running a farm. It never occurred to me that married non-farm women, spared rigorous physical labor, might be tired of their lives, even bored silly. Willis's idea of loosening the bonds that held us back seemed simple and obvious. My distillation of that idea was "women are people."

Still, a tiny voice told me to tread lightly. I decided to try out my concept on a friend of Jon's who fancied himself a radical. You'd think I'd lobbed a grenade into his shorts! He harrumphed off, couldn't even begin to discuss it. Even Jon initially rebelled. But, open-minded person that he was, he quickly came around to understanding the issues and never looked back—intellectually at least. Like every couple we had practical kinks to work out in our fifty-plus years of marriage, mostly over who did what. (He claimed to have a 5 percent mechanical aptitude, which took him off handyman duty permanently.)

I never imagined how threatening my little issue would be to men. I assumed that if you were against oppressing blacks or bombing tiny Southeast Asian countries, you were against oppressing women. It wasn't that simple. I had never burned a bra or even contemplated it, but with Jon's newspaper buddies I had become a "bra burner." One of them found it hysterically funny and threw it up at me at every turn. I didn't respond. It was an argument that couldn't be won—at least, not yet.

I was surprised that I had to sell this idea even to my women friends, although they turned out to be easier converts. We discovered that we each had little survival techniques. One friend told me how she could get through her housework by pretending she was the maid and was getting paid for it. One—that would be me—wasn't overly committed to housework in the first place.

I was reminded of my place when Darcy and I went to a department store to buy a shirt for Jon. The salesman, a nice older gentleman, asked me if I wanted to open an account. No one had asked me that before. If I could not be a journalist, at least I could have a charge account! He sent us to the credit office where we sat and were ignored for a long time. It was not to be. Didn't the salesman know that as a woman I could not have a charge account on my own?

Although charge accounts did not appear in the lexicon of the women's movement, this new movement had become a hot topic for women's magazines, and I snatched them up. In those days these publications offered a jarring juxtaposition of the prevailing, unreflective objectification of women in advertisements, which appeared in between articles written by the mothers of modern feminism, such as Gloria Steinem, Betty Friedan, and so many others. A typical ad in *Mademoiselle* magazine showed a young woman riding a bicycle built-for-two when the handsome young man riding behind her notices her DANDRUFF! "She's about to lose her back seat driver," the ad warns. "With Head and Shoulders she might have kept him."

A *Mademoiselle* cover sported the headline, "Women: The New Sex," with the words "HANDLE WITH CARE" written across a woman's face. Sara Lee offered a "Women's Liberation Coupon," good for seven cents off any of Sara Lee's Danish, dessert cakes, sweet cakes, or rolls; and it was even better for your morale—after all, "wouldn't you rather open up a cool freezer than a hot oven?"

Then along came Elizabeth Janeway, whose book, "Man's World, Woman's Place," influenced my thinking for all time. Her premise: All of life, including gender roles, is grounded in social mythology, not reality, which is why change is so difficult. Even though many women had paid jobs by this point, the prevailing myth still said that they belonged at home, because that is where male society needed to have them. It was a man's world, and woman's place was in the home.

Why, in 1969, were we still stuck in this quagmire? Shouldn't we have made more progress than this? Puzzled by how we got to this place I began researching the only women's history I knew: the suffrage movement, which began with the first women's rights convention in Seneca Falls, New York, in 1848. Back then, women couldn't vote, go to college, speak in their churches, get a job, or even keep their own property after marriage. The underlying theme was the same: Society kept women from achieving anything on their own. I would visit Seneca Falls, home to the Women's Rights National Historical Park, three times over the years.

Even in 1848, Elizabeth Cady Stanton, Susan B. Anthony, and their allies in the suffrage movement were not starting from scratch. Mary Wollstonecraft, an early feminist, wrote in 1792, "It is time to effect a revolution in female manners—time to restore women to their lost dignity and make them as a part of the human species."

Although Ellen Willis sparked my consciousness and recruited me to that revolution to "restore women to their lost dignity," for me—and I suspect for many women of that time—it was not a straight line. I went to one consciousness-raising session, in vogue at the time, and never went to another. Pushing women's rights against a wall of opposition was enough of a burden on my psyche without investing in the emotional trauma of strangers. And I had other things to do with my time, not the least of which was running a household and caring for a family.

I became a charter subscriber to *Ms. Magazine* in 1972, but I couldn't read it for years. I didn't dare expose myself to any more revolutionary ideas than were already simmering in my consciousness. I still have seventeen years' worth of the magazine in my basement.

Years later, when we were back in Minneapolis in the 1990s, I went to see Gloria Steinem at a bookstore where she was signing books. I handed her the inaugural issue of *Ms.* and asked her to sign it. She looked at the historic issue and said, "I hear this is worth one hundred dollars." I smiled and replied, "It's worth more now."

During my years in Grand Rapids I worked for women's rights, but I was never a radical. I shunned proposals for a total reorientation of society. And while the struggle for women's equality in the workplace struck very close to home, I had to turn my attention to another political battle, with more immediate life-and-death consequences, which concerned a bloody war that was raging in an obscure country on the other side of the world.

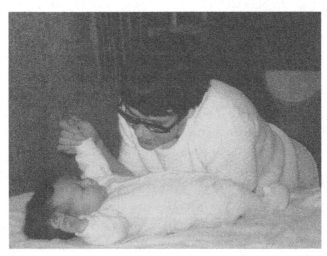

15. Being jobless in Grand Rapids gave me time to spend with my daughter, and to think about the role of women in America.

16. Jon batting, and Bruce Buursma pitching. In the summer, the Grand Rapids *Post* paid for them to enter a softball league. There were five male reporters in their twenties, a smoldering cauldron of testosterone.

17. George Hage, my J School mentor. When I told George that another male reporter had referred to one of my freelance pieces for the Grand Rapids *Press* as written by "any old housewife," George said, "You can write rings around him."

Chapter 11

Susie Logie is a beauty. At first that was a source of angst for a plain-Jane like me. She was the wife of a rising young lawyer and lived in a mansion—albeit crumbling—in Heritage Hill, Grand Rapids' historic neighborhood. I lived in a ramshackle rented house not far away. She was elegant; I was rumpled. But we soon discovered we were kindred spirits. We came out of a 1950s and 1960s culture that frowned on women stepping out of their roles as wives, mothers, and keepers of inviting homes. We were small town girls of whom little was expected. We shared a curiosity about life and its nuances, and a fierce will that we pulled from our psyches. We became friends for life.

Susie didn't rebel against the roles she was handed. She embraced them, even when the women's movement challenged those traditional roles. She wanted to be a wife and mother. Her devotion showed in the children she raised and in the historic home she restored. When she needed to find time for her art and for civic involvement, she stole time. Perfection was not in her toolbox, not with three children. "I never got everything done," she said. "I was robbing Peter to pay Paul."

Heritage Hill, where Susie has lived for fifty years, is a welcoming and industrious neighborhood. Susie organized a work group of neighborhood women of several generations to help each other make improvements on their old houses—each week working on a different house in turn. They stripped wallpaper, refinished and polished wood, scraped and sanded, and enjoyed the conversation as much as the progress. To preserve the city's heritage, she and two others made themselves "monument monitors" to keep the city's architectural history from being swept away.

Civic activists met frequently at her house to look for ways that Grand Rapids could move forward without destroying the good that was there. Inevitably, the talk would segue into the foibles of the human race, including local personalities, even entire genders. Susie's husband, John, didn't escape her irreverence: "John starts talking and then figures out what to say. I decide what I want to say first."

John was eventually elected mayor and served for twelve years, and she considered herself his partner. When he launched a campaign to raise $5 million to hire one hundred additional cops— a way to get police officers into neighborhoods—she wrote in a letter to me, "I'm for it, having thought it up."

She also wrote, "John is making a real difference in GR and in Michigan. I help him, of course, and then there's my stuff. I like and/or believe in all I/we do. Just can't figure out when to goof off." Much of "her stuff" was focused on justice, particularly for poor children in what was then called "the inner city."

When city commissioners wanted to eliminate four of the city's seven swimming pools, "it infuriated me," she said. She and friends descended on city hall—not once, but several times—wearing straw hats and flip flops, carrying towels, slathered in smelly coconut oil. She wanted their entrance to the city hall chamber to be multi-sensory: "I wanted them to not just see us. I wanted them to smell us coming." Unfortunately, the commissioners were not swayed, and the city eliminated the four pools that poor black children could walk to. It gussied up the three that remained and began charging admission.

Susie and a friend, Rebecca Hoffman, were regulars at city hall, where they raised such issues as downtown planning and historic preservation. City commissioners let her in, of course. She was pleasant and polite. They could usher her out, but they knew she'd be back. Susie imagined the dialogue balloon above their heads saying, "Her again?"

She also did something no one else dared to do in this staunchly conservative city, home to future president Gerald R. Ford: she organized a peace vigil. The Vietnam War was raging, and in the early 1970s it was the issue that overwhelmed all others. Only after

I graduated from college had I seen the atrocities of the war on television. Why were we, a superpower, killing innocent people in a small Asian nation? How could we justify the deaths of so many of our own young men?

Susie extended a hand to me when she started to organize a weekly silent vigil against the war in 1969. Susie and I were young mothers who raged against the killing of young men in Vietnam for a goal no one could articulate. This was a very conservative city, which made Susie's action daring, but we didn't care if anyone called us Commies, or worse, and they did.

The vigil was bold and out front. We held it every Thursday at noon on Calder Plaza, a central location, in full view of city government offices. At these events Susie and I, Doris Andersen, along with assorted young mothers, students, and octogenarian pacifists, spoke out against the war, raising tombstone-shaped signs that proclaimed, *"Not One More Son," "Not One More Gun,"* and *"Your Tax Dollars at Work,"* with an enlarged photo of the My Lai massacre.

The Grand Rapids *Press* mostly ignored us, even though we were visible from the newspaper's windows. Because Jon worked for the paper it would not publish my anti-war letters, so I wrote them and Susie signed them. Though we rarely got into the news columns, every week we ran a paid ad on the newspaper's front page which began with Henry Kissinger's quote, "Peace is at hand," and then gave the updated figures for the death count of soldiers from Kent County. As the months and years passed, and the death count rose, respect grew for our band of protesters who stood in a solemn line week after week.

When an occasional passersby thanked us for what we were doing at our vigil, we didn't accept their thanks graciously. We thought but didn't say, "If you're against the war, can't you stand with us for a half hour?" No, this was Grand Rapids, Michigan. Not a way to make yourself popular.

The vigil went on for three years, through blizzards and heat waves and police surveillance. An FBI agent who photographed us and our children knew we were members of the Women's International League for Peace and Freedom, a so-called radical leftist peace group dating back to World War I—an organization the feds had been monitoring for decades. Susie knew who this FBI agent was; she knew his name. She even let him into our meetings, where he not-so-subtly tried to get us to inform on Vietnam era "radicals." We declined.

For me this experience was transformative. If I couldn't work as a reporter, I could be part of something I felt strongly about. By inviting me to join her at the vigil Susie threw me a lifeline and drew me into her orbit.

§

All the while, Susie was raising children, hosting Thanksgiving gatherings at her home, and summer outings at her humble summer house in Charlevoix. She also engaged in an endless campaign to inject style into her Richardsonian Romanesque house. Built in 1892, it had been trashed and had no functioning utilities when she and John took up residence there in 1969. "I suffered from grandiosity in thinking 'there's nothing I can't do,'" she said about taking on this project. Susie is now eighty, and her house is a gem.

Creative in everything she did, Susie had set aside her painting for years, to make space for raising a young family and trying to end the war. As the vigil was nearing an end, she and John adopted a five-year-old Korean girl, Susannah, to join their young son John Jr. Shortly afterward, she became pregnant with daughter Libby! So it wasn't until the 1980s that she picked up on her art again, and in the afternoons, when the light was just right, she might be found painting from the downtown parking garage, or in neighborhoods all over Grand Rapids, painting streetscapes of the city. "When I put my creative endeavor first, nice things happen," she wrote to me about her painting. "The first and best nice thing is at the end of the day I've done something important, something very few people do. I've observed with maximum focus and demystified what I see. Since almost no one paints from life today, I know I'm having a rare treat."

Susie prefers painting from life "because of what the brain and hand are forced to learn. A building will stay the same all day and night, but the light will change, so you have to chase the light. That means you have two to two and a half hours maximum." Many of her paintings are available as posters or on canvas. I have one in my living room.

The most salient aspect of Susie's character is her capacity for friendship. She draws us in, makes us laugh and affirms us. When she needed help raking leaves, she invited friends to a "raking bee." No one showed up—except me. We had a ball!

When I left Grand Rapids in 1973, shortly before the vigil ended, I was a different person from the one who arrived there four years earlier. Working with Susie I learned that I didn't have to toe the line, any line. I knew I could be different. As I went on to a thirty-two-year journalism career in which I regularly questioned authority, I knew that even though Susie might be a thousand miles away, she had my back. "I think there's a romance to journalism," she would tell me. "There's sort of a nobility in doing it."

Our venue for communication over the years has been words on paper, sent through the mail; the lifeline Susie threw me was still attached through our letters. Susie often writes in pencil. Her letters are always entertaining. "I knew you hadn't abandoned this correspondence," she once wrote after a long silence from my end. "Almost nobody I know here maintains one, so I suspect we now have an elitist art form to maintain."

On my fiftieth birthday she returned all my letters to me. I returned hers on her seventieth. But first I read through them all again. I saw the same Susie I met so long ago, with a brilliant searching mind and openness to new ideas, strength of character and loyalty to friends, principled stands against injustice or just bad thinking, irreverence to power brokers and impatience with people who choose to live limited and unprincipled lives.

She's an unsung heroine, like the women whose untold stories I would seek out as a journalist. I've never met anybody like Susie Logie, and I never will again.

18. The Grand Rapids peace vigil was bold and out front. We held it every Thursday at noon on Calder Plaza, a central location, in full view of city government offices.

19. Susie Logie organized the Thursday vigil. At first, her beauty was a source of angst for a plain-Jane like me. But we soon discovered we were kindred spirits. We came out of a 1950s and 1960s culture that frowned on women stepping out of their roles as wives, mothers, and keepers of inviting homes.

Chapter 12

We were standing in Tony Brouwer's basement, a bunch of peace activists, when three male operatives from the New Democratic Coalition walked in. We weren't sure what these guys were up to, but after listening for a few minutes it soon became clear: They wanted to wrest control of the county Democratic Party from the United Auto Workers.

It was 1970 and the battle for the presidential nomination of the Democratic Party had one issue at its heart: who was ready, willing, and able to bring a speedy end to the Vietnam war. In Michigan, the leftist New Democratic Coalition (NDC), organized in opposition to the war, saw itself as the primary adversary of the UAW, the dominant political force in a state whose economy ran on automobiles. Though the UAW had done great things for its workers, it was thoroughly embedded in the establishment, had supported Lyndon Johnson as he led the country into the war, and was resistant to the kind of unapologetic anti-war candidate that the movement was crying out for.

The UAW had controlled the Democratic Party in Michigan for years, and only the UAW had the money to run Democratic campaigns in this Republican stronghold, home to future president Gerald R. Ford. But the local chapter of the Party in Grand Rapids was in a shambles, with no money and no office. It was ripe for a takeover, and the NDC wanted to swoop in and take over well in advance of the 1972 election. They decided to run some of our people—anti-war activists—as precinct delegate candidates against the UAW's people. As the craziness of this plan dawned on me, I thought, "I've never been involved in a coup before but Whee! First time for everything!"

Widespread disgust with the war in Vietnam had brought together many different kinds of people, so it wasn't surprising that this conspiratorial meeting took place in Tony Brouwer's lovely home on a leafy street at the edge of the city. In this solidly Republican, Dutch Calvinist stronghold Tony was Chairman of the Economics Department at Calvin College and a member of the Christian Reformed Church.

But he also was a rebel with portfolio: poverty, education, labor relations, and peace and justice for all. He had finely-honed political instincts and was willing to share them with people like us— neophytes with passion and idealism but little experience. So it was that we were in Tony's basement planning a coup.

The NDC leaders were all fired up to start the revolution, but when it came time to get the campaign organized the NDC boys— they were all males—decided, one by one, that training people to run for these positions was beneath their pay grade. They trotted their penny loafers out the door. That is how I entered politics: the last woman standing got to do the work.

I had, mind you, just found out in that meeting what a precinct delegate was. But I set my mind to making this happen. I read books. And then I talked to old-timers, who told me to disregard anything I read in the books. Drawing on Tony's know-how and experience I recruited candidates, educated them on how to run, and conducted classes for them in his basement.

I also ran myself, knocking on doors in my neighborhood— something I had learned to do years ago selling Christmas cards in Peterson. I beat my UAW opponent 34-21, and we elected a handful of delegates. It was a feeble start, but now we few, we pitiful band of political revolutionaries, were official members of the Party.

As the 1972 presidential year neared, I was eager to get involved in a campaign. At first I signed on with Maine Senator Edmund Muskie, the mainstream candidate, but soon joined my peace activist friends in the campaign of Senator George McGovern of South Dakota. His populist views were appealing to a daughter of neighboring Minnesota.

To get my name off the Muskie committee I called an NDC operative who'd signed on with Muskie. "If you organize precinct delegates for McGovern, I won't be able to hold the UAW back," he warned me. "They'll roll right over you." So, I thought, this is politics—a compatriot one day and a bully the next. What fun to think that Doris Andersen, Betsy Pullen, and I were such a threat to the established order! At first Doris and I juggled the McGovern campaign between our houses, taking turns caring for our five-year-olds; eventually we were able to rent a tiny storefront office. On primary day we elected sixty delegates for McGovern, more than any other candidate.

We traded our ramshackle campaign headquarters for proper offices and invited the UAW hierarchy to visit. I tried not to smirk as the guys who were supposed to roll over me sat in rank order and listened to our plans for the campaign. But as McGovern's campaign gathered steam nationally, it sent in young men to replace us. They sat at our dinner tables, talking to our husbands as if we weren't there. They fought over who would carry Shirley MacLaine's suitcase when the actress came for a campaign visit.

None of them offered to carry Shirley Chisholm's suitcase when she came to town as a presidential candidate. Chisholm was the first black woman elected to the U.S. Congress and the first African American to run for a major party's nomination for president. She once said, to my surprise, that being a woman was a worse handicap than being black. She came with a message that resonated with me, "If they don't give you a seat at the table, bring a folding chair." When I think back to that campaign, Shirley should have been my candidate. She was a woman of stature, and she was right on all of my issues, but I was too invested in my candidate to break out of the conventional mode I'd locked myself into.

When McGovern came to town for a rally I was outraged to see the NDC operative who had threatened me if I started to support McGovern sitting there on the stage. I went to the national campaign hierarchy and demanded to see McGovern personally. When I met with him that day, just the two of us in the basement of city hall, I found that I had little to say. I thanked him for his progressive politics, for his affirmation of us newcomers. I said that as a Minnesotan I enjoyed working for him, and that was about it. By that time the process had already soured me.

Still, I wasn't about to give up the big prize: the chance to become a delegate to the Democratic National Convention in Miami Beach. I entered the race to be a delegate and I prepared a campaign flyer, highlighted by Jon's ringing endorsement: "One of the really great broads of our time." It was an easy win.

Alice Vaughn and I were the "new breed" of delegate: she is black, I was twenty-seven years old. The Democratic Party, trying to clean up its disastrous mess at the 1968 convention in Chicago, had pledged to allocate half the seats to women in 1972, and we ended up being 38 percent, which was not half, but was a significant step forward.

We were participating in an important rite of national political life, we were serious, and we were intent on changing the course of our country in Vietnam, on civil rights, and on equal opportunities for women. But the media didn't know what to do with seven hundred women—they depicted us more as spectacle than serious participants. The Washington Post described Gloria Steinem as wearing "a body shirt and jeans," Marlo Thomas wore "a décolleté, bare midriff halter and jeans," and Shirley MacLaine "a dashiki and jeans." What were Norman Mailer and Abbie Hoffman wearing?— the papers had no comment. But what should I have expected? Before I left for Miami one of Jon's colleagues said to me, "My wife has her needlepoint, and you have your politics."

Only Nina Totenberg, writing in the now-defunct *National Observer*, saw the politics of 1972 for what it was: "Men have never been stingy about letting women share in the quadrennial rite of nominating presidential candidates. For their share the men took the important posts, the decision-making, the power, and the credit. They gladly gave women the errands, the telephoning, the stamp licking, the coffee serving, and the anonymity."

Still, it was exhilarating to be on the convention floor with the likes of Gloria Steinem, Betty Friedan, Coretta Scott King, Julian Bond, and Jessie Jackson. I dug in my purse to find a safety pin so Jimmy Breslin could attach his credentials. It was exhilarating, too, to be back in the place where the Reverend Martin Luther King Jr. gave me a map to live a maladjusted life, refusing to adjust myself to society's wrongs.

But the heady excitement was all over when our candidate, George McGovern, was forced to drop his chosen vice-presidential choice, Thomas Eagleton, when it was revealed that in the 1960s Eagleton had been hospitalized for depression and had undergone electroshock treatment. When word spread at the convention that the Eagleton candidacy was going to be a problem, I walked over to the Minnesota delegation, where I asked that dashing Norwegian American politician, Senator Walter Mondale, if he would step in to replace Eagleton. He graciously—and wisely—declined. When I told him I was a born Minnesotan though serving as a Michigan delegate, he smiled a big smile and said, "With a name like Halvorsen you'd have to be from Minnesota."

At the end of the convention, I was swept up in the tide of emotion as several thousand bodies—many wearing the mantle of political newcomer—swayed to "We Shall Overcome," the anthem of the disfranchised. But really, I was crushed. We women, despite our numbers, didn't seem to have accomplished anything. Our issues were lost in the turmoil over the ticket.

McGovern, of course, lost in a landslide to Richard Nixon. (We didn't know at the time that the political dirty tricks of Watergate would drive Nixon from office two years later, and he would be replaced by Michigan's own Gerald Ford.) I gave my heart and soul to the campaign, but by the time election night rolled around I could not bear to go to campaign headquarters.

§

Christmas was soon upon us, and Darcy was smitten by Santa Claus. She saw him five times, never noticing how different each of the Santas looked. But for a five-year-old she was a bit jaded about politics. After the election she asked why the McGovern office wasn't open anymore. "Because he's not running for president anymore," I explained. "But he is still a senator," I added by way of reassurance.

"And he's still a grandpa," she said. "But he's not president. He was going good until Mr. Stupid Nixon got ahead of him."

Admonition from Mom not to call the president names.

"Okay," she said, "but he's a mean man. He started the pollution, you know." You reap what you sow. Is it any wonder that Darcy grew up to become a Democratic activist?

Like my five-year-old daughter, I too was burned out on politics, but I still had one more political sortie left in me. After the election the leadership of the local Democratic Party had to be decided, and this was to be another struggle between the reformers and the old guard. The NDC guys, whose reform ideas had started this whole thing, and who lured me into politics, had gone over to the dark side. I was running the show as we "irregulars" tried to secure control of the Party after the election. A couple of principled attorneys, Dale Sprik and Gary Schenk, were still with us, and we met with them to strategize.

Then I went home to gather the tools of the trade: my credentials reports, *Robert's Rules of Order*, copies of the election laws, three hundred printed platforms, delegate list, and so forth. Hardly any of us knew *Robert's Rules of Order*, but I knew you could do anything you wanted in party politics if you had the votes. I put bacon and eggs on the table for Jon and Darcy and ran out the door just as the landlord was arriving to fix the plumbing.

Some of our delegates said they would not show up if we negotiated with the "regulars," and we needed everyone, so we had to duke it out the hard way. We tried an ingenious, extra-legal approach to seating delegates, and attempted other tactics that the regulars had never seen before. But in the end, we simply did not have the votes. We lost the chairmanship by two votes and the executive committee by one.

My political gig was over. And so was my sojourn in Grand Rapids. Jon, Darcy, and I moved the next day. If we had stayed I might have run for office, now that I knew how to do it. As we prepared to leave, I still had hopes of getting a job in journalism, but my days of unemployment, it turned out, were good for all of us. Darcy thrived in those important early years. Jon found success and camaraderie in his first job as a reporter. I experienced a life I would never have again, as a young mom and activist. And I made lifelong friends.

The girl from Peterson had sampled the giddiness of power. I got to tell a state legislative candidate, "No, I won't run your campaign." (The real message was, "I don't help power-hungry young narcissists who haven't learned to tie their shoes yet.") I got to tell a party official, who called to find out how he could become a delegate, "Sorry, party rank has no clout this year." I got to tell a young UAW emissary, when he said they were going to remove me from the county committee, "Go ahead. And tell the boys I appreciate the compliment."

I didn't give any thought to being a leader. I was too busy being one. But eventually a tiny Norwegian spark went off in my brain: You have been affirmed as a leader. I didn't extinguish it. I'm convinced that all of this experience helped me later as a reporter; for example, telling an arrogant Minneapolis judge who was minimizing me, "I've spent more time in courtrooms than you have."

And my days in Grand Rapids got me into the history books, earning me a listing in *The Political Graveyard*, "the internet's most comprehensive source of U.S. political biography," which offers a listing of over 277,483 politicians, living and dead. My citation informs us that I am "still living as of 1972."

20. Darcy and I enjoy a doughnut excursion at a Grand Rapids park.

21. Julian Bond and Jesse Jackson at the 1972 Democratic National Convention in Miami.

22. Me at the Grand Rapids peace vigil, which was the prelude to my political activism.

23. Betty Freidan at the DNC.

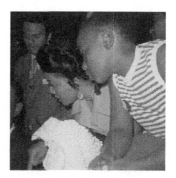

24. Coretta Scott King at the DNC.

25. Columnist Jimmy Breslin.

26. Gloria Steinem at the DNC.

Chapter 13

N ext stop: Albany, New York, where Jon was hired by the Associated Press. I still had the idea that this was a profession that didn't want me, but I applied for a job because I couldn't give up on my dream. In those days it was standard practice to put "family status" on your resume, so the newspapers knew I had a child. I wondered if "family status" was actually a cousin to "nepotism," another way of excluding women.

When the *Times Union* called with a job offer, I was surprised. This was my first professional reporting job, and I was both thrilled and astonished to go to work for the major paper in New York's capital city. Had things miraculously gotten better for women in the six years since I graduated? No, not really, as I discovered by the total lack of childcare when I started to work. Just the year before Richard Nixon had vetoed a comprehensive childcare bill, calling it "communal child-raising."

In the years that followed I wondered if I could trace my hiring to the young Managing Editor, Bern Zovistoski, who maybe didn't see motherhood as the cultural barrier that the older guys did. Or maybe he thought it wasn't the newspaper's business, an attitude that was a long way from getting traction at most workplaces.

It was 1973. I was twenty-eight, old for a rookie, but needless to say I was delighted to get to work. My first assignment was to cover two small Hudson River communities: Green Island was a tranquil island town along the Hudson River, and Cohoes an old industrial city a little further north. Soon I bought my first car, a light blue VW bug.

I liked being off on my own, poking about, finding stories. I loved working with people and with words to put stories together. My notebook served as a mask for my shyness, my job a shy but curious person's dream. And I loved getting it right, which frightened me a bit now that I was in the real world, with thousands of people reading what I wrote—in New York state, of all places.

Green Island had little news, but Cohoes produced a lot, and I did what all beat reporters do: I was assigned to cover city council meetings, check-in with the police department and city hall, and write feature stories when I found them. I even had my own seat at weekly Rotary Club meetings, which seemed odd at first but turned out to be very useful. If someone didn't return my phone calls I knew I could find him at Rotary—these guys took their Rotary obligations seriously.

The people in these small towns were mostly receptive to me, which was a relief because I had found that Albany itself was not "Minnesota nice" like my home state. The first day I left our apartment I was snapped at by a grocery store clerk and honked at by a trucker, but that was the little stuff.

Corruption was woven into the city's fabric, and there was no attempt to hide it. Mayor Erastus Corning II had already been mayor for thirty years when I arrived and would retain that position until his death in 1983. Together with Democratic Party boss Daniel P. O'Connell he ran the most powerful political machine in the country, and one of the longest lasting in American history.

When cops were found to be stealing coins from parking meters, it was barely a blip on the city's radar. Albany residents knew where they stood. "I'd vote for a dog if he were a Democrat," our landlord said as he painted the back porch. There were more Democrats under indictment in Albany than there were Democrats in all of Grand Rapids.

"Being a reporter in this vicious political atmosphere is like being a dartboard," I wrote to Susie Logie. "Public officials lie to you to see if you'll swallow whatever choice morsel they're offering up, then boast afterward about how they've deliberately misled you. But I take the fact that I've made a certain number of enemies as an indication that I'm doing my job."

That atmosphere permeated the area, and it intensified as federal Model Cities money flowed into old Eastern Rust Belt cities and other communities in need of urban renewal. I always saw myself as a feature writer, and never thought I'd find myself investigating corruption on my first job. But I also never imagined that the small city of Cohoes would be swept up in allegations of misusing federal money.

I didn't uncover this story, but I was assigned to cover it, and it was nasty. A lot was at stake for the city and its employees, and people were reluctant to talk. I developed a source who was a state employee, well connected in Cohoes politics, who became my own Deep Throat. He knew everything. We talked daily. Another source, a Cohoes city employee, I had to meet far outside the city to avoid being seen. I also had evidence that I was being watched. One night someone went through the glove compartment of my car outside our apartment. Then someone turned on the water outside our building at five in the morning. I went down from our second-floor apartment to turn it off. I was too sleepy to consider that someone might be waiting for me with a baseball bat; no one was, but it was harassment in keeping with the nastiness of the investigation. It was aimed at me because I was the driving force behind this story.

Paul Van Buskirk, the main object of the investigation, grew up in Cohoes and graduated with an engineering degree from prestigious Rensselaer Polytechnic Institute in next-door Troy. But he was drawn to politics. He was a shrewd political operative who created the Cohoes Citizens Party in 1963 and used it as a vehicle to wrest control of city hall from the Albany Democratic machine.

Van Buskirk ran the mayoral campaign of Dr. James McDonald in 1963 and after he won, he became his executive assistant. When McDonald died of a brain tumor his wife, Virginia McDonald, served out the remaining two years of his term. Van Buskirk then ran her for mayor and he served as campaign manager. She won that election and appointed Van Buskirk as head of the newly formed Planning and Development Agency, which had oversight of the Model Cities program.

A number of civic improvements were made with Model Cities money—the Music Hall was restored and a church converted into a city library, to name just two. But Model Cities also had a housing renovation program for which, by Van Buskirk's own admission, the rules were loose. It was in that program that accusations of mismanagement were first made concerning Van Buskirk and the Neighborhood Improvement Program's director, which I reported. It was alleged that building materials charged to one project weren't used there. It was also alleged that improvements were made on property owned by Van Buskirk.

Detractors also said that while he was a city employee he was employed as a consultant to an area firm that received $100,000 in contracts with Cohoes. He maintained that his work for that firm was on out-of-state projects. Mayor Virginia McDonald, Van Buskirk's close friend, hired an outside firm to investigate the allegations but nothing ever came of it.

In the end, Van Buskirk was done in by his own party. His most severe critics were Citizens Party members who said he had become like the autocratic Albany machine politicians their party had routed from Cohoes politics. Van Buskirk was never charged with any crimes but after a string of revelations in the press, he resigned on January 7, 1974. He cited the pressures of his job and "malignant abuses" by his opponents. He criticized two Citizens Party members by name.

On the day he was to announce his resignation one of his cohorts left a message for me giving the wrong location for the press conference. This was probably an attempt at retribution for the stories I had been publishing, but I already knew where the press conference would be and I arrived in good time. "We're still thinking of suing you," his lawyer said to me afterward. I looked him in the eyes and replied, "Go ahead." I may have been a rookie, but I had journalism school chops. I knew it was a bluff.

27. City Editor Bob McManus, seated left, and Managing Editor Bern Zovistoski, standing. These two helped me to thrive at my first job as a reporter.

28. Lifting weights at the Cohoes police department.

29. Darcy's first day of school in Albany.

30. I was always tugging at my hair in the newsroom. One of the photogs took this one of me.

Chapter 14

O utside of work in Albany a lovely thing happened: Dad and I rediscovered—and reclaimed—his music. When my parents visited us in the places where we lived, I always looked for special things for them to do. Just before Dad was to leave at the end of his Albany visit I found something truly special: a bluegrass festival.

As Jon, Dad, Darcy, and I climbed a hill toward a tiny wooden stage in the woods outside of Albany, we heard the kind of music I grew up with. It had authenticity and a joy that I hadn't heard in music for a long time. I had given up on country in the 1960s when it went commercial and lost its rural soul. I was smitten by rock 'n' roll as a teen, but tuned out most of that, too.

As the acoustic sounds of fiddle, banjo, mandolin, bass, and guitar seeped through the woods, it seemed close to the music Dad had played for years. I tried to gauge the look on his face. It seemed like wonder.

As a child I really had no choice but to hear old-time country music. My dad's band, the Root River Ramblers, practiced in our house in Peterson on Friday nights in the 1950s.

Then I found out, somehow, that the same music came over the radio on Saturday nights. So I got Dad to find the station for me, and I put my seven-year-old ears close to our big box radio and listened to the likes of Ernest Tubb, Kitty Wells, and Hank Williams. I could hear them only on clear nights when the Grand Ole Opry's signal came in from Nashville. When it didn't, I listened to the National Barn Dance from Chicago.

Some were classic drinking songs, or songs of lost love or betrayal, or they were about trucks, trains, and mama. But other songs told true stories, such as Hank Snow's "Blind Boy's Dog," about people who donated their dogs to the military in World War II. I wasn't able, in my tender years, to decide whether any of the lyrics I heard were suitable for a kid, nor could I necessarily make them out. (My ears didn't work very well.) I just wanted that sound that I heard in my living room on Friday nights.

At age twelve or so Dad learned to play the fiddle that his grandfather had brought from Norway and his father had played before him. It was a precious thing—no one was supposed to touch it. But Dad took it down from the wall and taught himself to play. He became renowned as a fiddler, and the music he played was much in demand in nearby towns.

Dad was something of a local celebrity in those days, playing at dances and in taverns, and winning talent contests again and again. The band also had a show on WKTY Radio in La Crosse, Wisconsin on Saturday mornings. I put my ear up close to the radio for that too.

Eventually the band broke up, and the prized Norwegian fiddle sat idle for years, especially after Dad's hands and shoulders became arthritic. But I restored his music to both of us when I took him to that first bluegrass festival near Albany in 1975.

We lost the music, for a time, when we moved to Arizona, but when we moved to Portland, Maine, in 1977, I found another festival. That first summer Dad and I set off for Smokey Greene's festival on a farm in upstate New York, a six-hour trip from Portland. Dad, Jon, and I would make that journey many times after that, pitching our tent in an idyllic spot in the foothills of the Adirondack Mountains. From 6:00 P.M. to midnight that first day music flowed from a tiny stage. It was a combination of bluegrass, a growing but still mostly cult roots music, and the old-time country music of the 1940s and 1950s.

Dad didn't make it to midnight. It was cold, as it often would be there in August, but as he headed to the tent I burrowed into a sleeping bag in front of the stage, covering even my head, and held out until the final jam session. This was the best part of the festival, when all the musicians crowded onto the stage and played such rousing songs as "Will the Circle Be Unbroken?" and "The Orange Blossom Special." I stayed till the end, under the influence of nothing but the cold night air—a lump on the ground, with light snow falling on me.

There was no warmth to be found that first night. The temperature dropped to thirty-eight degrees, but it didn't deter the "parking lot pickers," who had come to play as much as to listen. They moved from one campsite to another, playing until nearly dawn. By 6:00 A.M. the rains came, and the roof of our tent sagged with water. I punched the water out and put on bacon to fry and coffee to perk. With another cold night in store, Dad and I went to Saratoga Springs and found a motel room. Then we returned to the festival, where the sun warmed us and the stage came alive again at noon.

There weren't many festivals in the 1970s, but the music was catching on. Kentuckian Bill Monroe created this acoustic roots music in the 1940s by melding old-time country with the traditional music brought by the English, Scots, and Irish to the hills of southern Appalachia in the eighteenth century. Like old-time country, it was a story-telling music with laments about hard lives and lost love, but it set itself apart by its fast pace and instrumental virtuosity.

Smokey Greene's was one of the early festivals, and Smokey kept it going for years. Born into a musical family in Vermont during the Great Depression, he taught himself to play nearly every instrument as a teenager and became an icon of country music. He was not a nut about bluegrass, he told me, but an old-time country guy whose favorite performer was Ernest Tubb. Add a banjo to an Ernest Tubb song, he said, and you have bluegrass. But he played country straight up, singing the songs of the 1940s and 1950s that nobody much played anymore, songs like "Just Plain Folks," with a whiskey baritone much like Tubb's, to the delight of his fans.

He never made it big in the country music business, though he was funny and charismatic and as big a star as you could be without going to Nashville. He had a huge fan club whose members sent him cards when he was sick, though he was healthy and still performing into his late eighties.

Jon was a rock fan who would have fled a bluegrass festival if given a chance to go to a Bruce Springsteen show instead, but he came to love these festivals. They were a highly pleasurable event for him—authentic, often exhilarating, with music performed in the open air by "just folks," and heard by just folks, accompanied by a pervasive neighborliness that seemed out of sync with the times.

I began writing about bluegrass for the Portland papers as a sideline to my regular job, simply because nobody else was doing it. It was a cultural phenomenon, a slice of Americana that I thought might be interesting to almost anybody. Far from the Appalachian south, Maine had festivals and performers who played for the joy of it, not to become known. I wrote about many of the shining lights of New England bluegrass: Fred Pike, Bob and Grace French, Mac and Hazel McGee, Sam Tidwell, Al Hawkes, Kendall Morse and others. And, of course, Smokey, who was a regular at Maine festivals.

As we were driving home to Maine after that first New York festival, Dad said what he'd probably been thinking all weekend: that if he'd had the money for instruments, he would have organized a family band back in Peterson. But we four kids, it seemed, lacked the musical genes that had been handed down from his Norwegian grandfather to his father to him. He did send Verdon and me to accordion lessons, and I have a recording of me playing "The Blue Skirt Waltz," a reminder of those days.

Dad came east from Minnesota each summer to go to one of these festivals with us for about half a dozen years, and the tapes he made of the music gave him pleasure during long Minnesota winters. Getting to know bluegrass, and Smokey Greene in particular, improved the quality of his life, and ours.

On frosty nights in South Portland I would have loved to listen to Dad playing with his old band. After he died my siblings and I searched everywhere, but all of his recordings have been lost.

31. Smokey's Annual Bluegrass Festival in upstate New York.

32. My dad listening to Bluegrass. His band, the Root River
Ramblers, practiced in our house in Peterson on Friday nights
in the 1950s.

33. Smokey Greene.

34. After publishing the most important story of my career up to that time, a triple shooting, Managing Editor Bern Zovistoski wrote, "Your performance in gathering, interpreting, and writing the stories on the triple shooting in Cohoes December 31 was simply out-standing. This is especially so because of the pressure you faced with an early New Year' s Eve deadline. You are a conscientious, talented, and tireless reporter and a credit to your profession, and it's a pleasure to have you on our staff."

Chapter 15

mong my daily duties at the *Times Union* I was responsible, along with another reporter, for filling a suburban news page three days a week. Since the community that he covered did not produce much news, I usually ended up finding and writing the stories to fill those pages. The long hours, the night meetings, the pressure to produce, our awful experiences with childcare, began to take a toll on my health. I was working way too hard, and as my health problems increased, it became more than I could handle. After a year and a half, I felt I'd aged five years.

"Since I've been working, I've more and more realized the virtue of just being home with a child of Darcy's age or younger," I wrote to Susie. "Not only are you there to handle problems the way you think they should be handled and see to it that they're eating decent food, but it provides a certain stability. Darcy seems to be thriving despite it all. One of us is with her much of the time because of our different schedules, but from her point of view I can see how things could be better if I were not working." I realized that I was done in by the pressure and demands of the job, and reluctantly, I quit.

It was summer, and it was good to be home with Darcy when she was out of school. I didn't have to worry about entertaining her. She was a magnet—she drew kids to her, just as she had in Grand Rapids. Day after day all the kids on our street trooped to our small apartment where Darcy ran a "school" in her bedroom. She was, of course, the teacher. I thought she was being overbearing with her "students," so I told her she could be the teacher only every other day. She reorganized the administration of the school by assigning two of her students to be teachers, and she hung a shingle that said, "Darcy Halvorsen, Principal."

Leaving the *Times Union* was a good and necessary breather at that moment. As my stomach problems settled down and a new school year approached, I began to think about working again. I had a job offer from the state Health Department but decided I couldn't give up on journalism so easily. The *Times Union* took me back as a general assignment reporter, a day job that was easier to handle. I covered my first murder trial, and sitting in the courtroom made me realize how difficult it was to hear in certain settings.

I found my own stories, including one on juvenile crime, which was rampant in the suburbs. I began by interviewing the police chief in Colonie, Albany's biggest suburb. It couldn't be easy admitting you had a problem with kids and crime, especially in the politically-charged climate of Albany—you didn't want the Democratic autocracy to come down on you because you couldn't control your local teenagers.

On this story I got my first inkling that men expected women reporters to be "nice," that we weren't like the hard-nosed newshounds who were out to get them. Powerful men thought that we would protect them and put the best possible spin on their stories. But as the chief sprawled, spread-legged, in a huge recliner, he said some things he shouldn't have, such as, "We shouldn't say that because it would give ammunition to our opponents." I didn't have to quote that in my story, but I did, in retaliation for so brazenly displaying his crotch. He was livid when the story appeared. Why did the chief decide to talk to me at all? Because he thought he could control me, he thought I'd be nice to him, he thought he'd get ahead of the other suburbs that were having the same problem.

My next story from Colonie began early one morning when an editor called me at home to send me to the scene of a possible double homicide. When I arrived on the scene it turned out that a couple had been overcome by carbon monoxide in their car, but they were still alive, and were going to be okay. By the time the cops arrived I had interviewed everybody, my work was done. This did not go over well with the police; I might have sabotaged a crime scene, they complained. Was it my fault the cops took so long getting to a scene where two people might be dead?

The biggest story I covered in my remaining days in Albany was a triple shooting in Cohoes, where a gunman shot and killed a mail carrier, then walked into the police station and opened fire, wounding two cops. The paper sent me because I knew the ropes in Cohoes. A police shooting was a big story and it felt great having better sources and knowing more than the reporter from the New York *Times*.

The shooter was an unemployed former postal employee named Martin Jubic. He was forty-two years old and had never been in serious trouble. The events were sudden and violent and after he opened fire in the police station one officer tackled him from behind while another grabbed his Winchester rifle. His motive was mysterious, though some speculated that he was inspired by a sniper who had killed three people in another small New York town three days earlier. "The answer," a police spokesman said, "may never be known." A jury found Jubic not guilty by reason of insanity.

The shooting took place on New Year's Eve Day, and it was past deadline when I returned to the office to write it up. I was so busy that I had to tell Jon, who was reporting the story from the AP bureau upstairs, that I couldn't help him. It was routine practice for newspaper reporters to help out their colleagues from the wire services, but in this case, I had to stiff my husband.

This story stood out as the biggest challenge of my young career. Bern Zovistoski wrote afterward, "Your performance in gathering, interpreting, and writing the stories on the triple shooting in Cohoes December 31 was simply outstanding. This is especially so because of the pressure you faced with an early New Year's Eve deadline. You are a conscientious, talented, and tireless reporter and a credit to your profession, and it's truly a pleasure to have you on our staff."

Years later I tracked him down. I wanted to find out why he hired me—twice. He replied, "You presented yourself as someone sincerely interested in journalism, and I sensed you were committed. Your family situation didn't rise to any level of concern; after all, I had two young children at home, and I knew the challenges that had to be dealt with in that regard. Furthermore, you totally redeemed yourself as a reporter, time and again."

We would remain in Albany for another year, and the gastrointestinal problems that would dog me the rest of my life became serious enough that I underwent testing. The doctors didn't find anything wrong, so they prescribed two potent tranquilizers, lithium and valium. These were the days when women's health problems were "in our heads," and doctors prescribed these magic pills to women for almost everything back then. We just needed to be calmed down. The first day I took the pills I thought I was supposed to take them every three hours, not three times a day, and by late afternoon I was all but passed out over my typewriter. I drove myself home—how, I don't know—and threw the pills away.

Altogether we stayed in Albany only two and a half years, it was a good career beginning. I discovered that most New Yorkers are not aloof or nasty, contrary to Midwestern perceptions. The place that gave me my first job was warm and welcoming. City Editor Bob McManus was a gem, putting up with my foibles. When we left, colleague Carol DeMare gave us a going away party. On my last day Bern said he would hire me a third time if he had the opportunity. He did, in fact, offer me a job again, but I had to turn him down.

It was a stunning affirmation, and I would have left Albany in a glow except for one big thing: Our time in Albany was difficult for a little girl who was used to having her mom around, and for a mom who realized, no matter what the women's movement told her, or what she told herself, that she couldn't have it all—at least not without a little help from a society that told her she belonged at home.

As we neared Christmas with Jon's parents, Jon reminded Darcy that she had to be good if she wanted Santa to come. She retorted, "Well, I saw him the other day at the mall and he said, 'I hope you get a lot of nice presents,' and he didn't say nuthin' about being good."

Chapter 16

e were in the midst of what I called our Wanderlust Tour. Jon was an adventurer, a wanderer, and if he had a chance to explore someplace new, he took it, with my waning acquiescence as I grew weary of setting up households and acclimating Darcy to new places. In some places, such as Phoenix, Arizona, and Portland, Oregon, we didn't stay long, but my mom, Evelyn, had a chance to visit us in Arizona. She may not have been happy that I left Minnesota, but she was eager to visit us on our wanderings.

Mom never had a chance to travel. She'd been a caretaker since she left school in the seventh grade to look after her mother, Grandma Marie to us kids, and she continued to be a caretaker while raising four children. Even after we were grown and had families of our own, Mom still looked after us, keeping us stocked with homemade bread. When Grandma Marie moved to Peterson later on, my mother visited her every day after work.

She was a good daughter and raised me to be one. She looked after others, too. She gave bread to everyone, always helped her neighbors, and for years she and a friend made Peterson's Memorial Day dinner and served it to hundreds. When she moved from Peterson to the Good Shepherd assisted living complex in Rushford, she gave her elderly neighbors rides or got their mail.

I was the eldest daughter—Nancy is seven years younger—the one who in many cultures is her mother's helper. As a little girl, I helped her deliver hot noon meals to Dad at the fish farm where he worked for a time; put up playbills for his country band; got up at 5:00 a.m. on Sunday morning to help her run her brother's restaurant (I was the pint-sized waitress); went with her to the 6:00

35. Mom, with Darcy, in Arizona.

a.m. Easter breakfast at the church; helped her carry ten-gallon milk cans of water from a neighbor's spigot when our pipes froze. Unlike most Peterson women, Mom also had a job, as a cook and waitress. She was renowned for her cooking—especially for making the best pies for miles around.

She wasn't one to brag, but once she started traveling, she must have been proud to tell her neighbors about her trips. "Where are you going next, Evelyn?" they would ask. She especially liked Arizona, which was exotic for a Minnesotan, with its mountains and deserts and warm winter air. And it brought her together with family. She got to spend time with her granddaughter Darcy, and Jon's parents also lived there, and they were generous and welcoming hosts. We all went sightseeing, ate two-pound steaks on a mountain top, and had a grand time.

Mom was brokenhearted when we left Minnesota and for years I wondered if she forgave me for abandoning her. I had been her helper, and I wasn't there anymore. But after she died, at age seventy-seven, she twice came to me in a dream and patted me on the shoulder as if to say, "It's okay." That was at a time when I was taking a sleep medication and never dreamed, or at least wasn't aware of dreaming, but it was very real to me.

At her funeral the minister recalled Evelyn's generosity and community spirit, and he added, "To the sons, daughters and grandchildren gathered here today, I want you to know she was proud of you and loved you."

The Christmas before she died she sent Darcy a card saying, "I have a lot of respect for you. You are so nice to everybody." It was the best compliment she could have paid anyone, and it made me feel good. I had raised a good daughter. Knowing that she felt that way and remembering the joy she found in her visits to see the seemingly exotic places where we lived, it brought about healing.

Chapter 17

fter our pit stops in Arizona and Oregon, we finally got it right: we moved all the way across the country from Portland, Oregon to Portland, Maine, where Jon was hired by the Associated Press. The city's three Gannett newspapers interviewed me, and I was waiting to hear when an *Evening Express* editor called me early one morning asking if I'd come in to handle a sensitive story: the suicide of an eleven-year-old girl.

Laura ———————————
She Needed Help, Time Ran Out

> The night before, Laura asked for a special pair of pants to be washed out for school and she worked on her homework. In the morning she dawdled over picking out earrings. At school she complained of a stomachache, left school and went to the Thornton Heights Church, where she took her life.

Officials at Laura's school knew she had deep-rooted emotional problems and were convinced she needed to be placed in a residential treatment facility, but time ran out. Complaining of a stomachache, she left school at noon, went to a church and killed herself, using a thirty-eight-caliber pistol she found at home.

I don't know why they called me in—maybe it was that I was a woman, and I had worked on the major paper in New York's capital—but I was apprehensive. I knew there had been a gun in the home, so when I went to interview the girl's mother, I asked another reporter to go with me. We left the interview with many unanswered questions. It was an era when people with mental illness were being moved out of institutions and into the community, and Maine had closed the state's only children's psychiatric hospital several years earlier. Some argued that hospitalizing children would stigmatize them and probably would do more harm than good. But now there was simply no place to put a child in crisis until longer-term help could be found. Perhaps a young girl killing herself was not envisioned as a possibility.

"I can be—but most of the time am not—a hard-nosed journalist, and this story tore me apart," I wrote to Susie in Grand Rapids. "An eleven-year-old suicide victim—how much more painful a story could there be? There were those who said we shouldn't have 'dragged it up,' that this was a private tragedy that should be left alone. But we thought society ought to know why children were killing themselves."

There was another reason why this story struck close to home: at the time Darcy was eleven.

I felt incredible anguish that this girl was hurting so much that she saw suicide as her only option. What terrible things had she experienced in her young life? Was there any way to keep this from happening to another child? How to help troubled kids was a long-standing issue in Maine but, without a tragic story like Laura's, it seemed to lack urgency.

I told myself afterward that if I were asked to do that story again I would not do it—yes, it was a powerful story for a young journalist, but it also was painful, especially for the mother of an eleven-year-old. It was shocking to me that so many children endured so much pain, largely invisible to the rest of us, and I could not turn my back on them. As this tragedy played out I wrote many follow-up stories on troubled kids, and I wrote about hunger and other issues affecting children. The local mental health agency gave me an award for those stories and for my reporting on a controversial proposal to build a private psychiatric hospital. But nothing I did could bring back this forsaken child.

When I was assigned to the court beat a year later, it became clear that I didn't have to give up covering such issues. They were right there in the courts. Increasingly, I saw the social virtues of a reporter's work, how we can illuminate issues as no one else can. By telling stories, we could peel back layers of the social fabric to find out why society continued to tolerate such atrocities as rape, domestic violence, child abuse, child sexual abuse, and the mental illness that is embedded in so many of these issues. One major reason, I concluded, was that the stories of victims were seldom told. What I found is that our reporting serves to enforce cultural norms by showing how perpetrators are punished for violating society's rules. But in our focus on the perpetrators, we let the victims slip into the shadows, their pain never acknowledged.

§

I didn't always seek out these types of stories—sometimes they came to me. The issue of child sexual abuse came to me in the person of Ron Allanach, a police officer in the Portland suburb of Westbrook, population 15,000, who had made it his mission to deal with the unrecognized pain of children in his community.

Allanach, a former social worker, spent a lot of time in local schools as his department's Officer Friendly. Children came to know him, so they listened when he talked about good touches and bad touches. It was 1978 when Ron approached me and it would be years before child sexual abuse would erupt into the national crisis it became. Meanwhile, children in Westbrook and elsewhere suffered enormous harm from the deviant behavior that was a deep, dark secret within their families and within society.

After only a few sessions, children started coming to Allanach saying they had been molested by someone, usually a family member or close adult friend. "I was first shocked, but then I realized the power I had as a police investigator to help kids, and to bring offenders to justice," Allanach told me.

When the three-year-old girl came into the district attorney's office to tell her story, she crawled under a table and refused to come out. Victim advocate Jim Conley lured her out with crayons. After she had colored a while, he brought out an anatomically correct doll, and she began to tell him what had happened to her. She went before a grand jury, and the man who sexually abused her was indicted.

Another girl was abused by her stepfather when she was eleven. When he came to court five years later, she wanted him to go to jail, and he did. Though the girl wanted her stepfather to be punished, she also was "a little bit afraid of him," said Assistant District Attorney Maryellen Black. She said it is important for the perpetrator to know that sex abuse is a crime, and for the child to know that it wasn't her fault. These outcomes became possible only after Ron Allanach brought the sexual abuse of children into the open in the Portland area.

The project exploded from the eight or nine cases a year police had previously seen. Allanach no longer thought, as he did initially, that he was being intrusive. "I saw the faces of children who no longer felt alone, who now had a defender, someone they could trust. This sense gave me immense energy."

The cases started to take over his office, his thinking, and his life. He and juvenile officer Charlotte Adams turned their office into a trauma center to handle interviews, court proceedings, emotional support, transportation, and housing for victims. "When the call comes in, it's like five thousand pounds of pressure on your head just like that," Allanach said. "You have to respond immediately."

"In all of this—and I never saw it coming—the important truth was that if this much was happening in this small town, child sexual abuse had to be widespread across the country," he said. "Yet in those days few, if any, wanted to talk about it, let alone do something about it. No one wanted to upset the status quo, to ask tough questions that could lead to a lot of trouble for many people, to turn the content existence of a small town into a troubling and disturbing nightmare—that their children were hurting, being abused. Many were suffering from a self-imposed public blindness of the truth."

Because of his work, that blindness slowly gave way to light in the Portland area. Police, prosecutors, courts, state agencies, and schools began to work together, and kids were starting to be believed. The Maine State Police created a squad of detectives to deal with the issue and engaged Allanach to provide training. He organized a national conference on the issue that he saw as the culmination of his work. Not until then did politicians come on board, he said. "The conference became a catalyst."

But the work was taking a toll on him. The State Police decided that detectives on its new squad should be rotated every three years because of that toll. Allanach had been at it for eleven years. He gave speeches, conducted training, carried out his police duties, and worked with children in the schools. Kids and families were relying on him. So was the community. But he couldn't keep up the pace much longer. He applied for the police chief's job and got it.

My stories put only a small spotlight on a huge issue, but Allanach said they "provided a framework in the Portland Metro area from which the philosophy for enforcement and protection followed. The stories provided a dedicated look before the story was fashionable."

But without Ron Allanach there would have been no stories. His attention to this difficult issue brought him nightmares and tears, but it made a difference. He created a program from scratch that became a model for other cities, dealing with an issue that soon would explode in places large and small all over the country. His work may have begun in a small town, but his influence was enormous.

36. Mom in Maine. Mom was brokenhearted when we left Minnesota and for years I wondered if she forgave me for abandoning her. I had been her helper, and I wasn't there anymore. But after she died, at age seventy-seven, she twice came to me in a dream and patted me on the shoulder as if to say, "It's okay."

37. Dad cooking. As a little girl, I helped Mom deliver hot noon meals to Dad at the fish farm where he worked for a time, and I put up playbills for his country band.

Chapter 18

J ody Gould's story was an American shame. At nineteen she was raped and beaten in broad daylight near her home in Portland. She could have collapsed into herself and let go of this crime because it was too hard to keep reliving it, but she stood fast for a year, until a jury convicted her attacker and sent him to prison.

"I did that—me!" she said afterward. "Sometimes I feel that was my mission in life. I was put here to put that guy away." Jody told her story on the front page of Portland's afternoon newspaper, allowing the use of her name and a photo at a time when rape was a deep, dark shame, when our culture told its victims "it's your fault."

Three years later the issue erupted nationally with a different victim, Nancy Ziegenmeyer, who was twenty-seven when she was raped in Des Moines, Iowa. She told her story to reporter Jane Schorer, opening up the black box of rape to a wide audience. "Rape is an American shame," the Des Moines *Register* proclaimed. "Our society needs to see that and attend to it, not hide it or hush it up." The story, published in 1990, won a Pulitzer Prize and put the issue of rape on the national stage.

Jody was attacked the day before she was to graduate from high school. Nobody told her she should break the taboo against speaking publicly about her rape. It was 1987, and that idea wasn't on the radar yet. But somehow, in the depths of her young soul, she found the fortitude to do it, stunning readers—and me—with her courage.

As the paper's court reporter, I covered her assailant's sentencing and began my story with a quote from her. She called the next day to thank me, saying she didn't think what she had to say was important. I responded that victims' stories need to be told and if she wanted to tell hers, I would like to hear it. Five months later I tracked her down and she agreed to tell her story. She came into the newsroom on a November afternoon and we talked for two hours. When darkness began to fall she became jittery and said she had to leave. The next day we talked for two more hours. While she didn't hesitate to let us use her full name and photo, she was nervous enough about it that she didn't tell her mother what she was doing.

Portland Police Detective Peter DeRice said the rape and beating were the most vicious he had investigated in his nineteen years on the police force. In broad daylight, as Jody walked along railroad tracks in a marshy area near her home, a man jumped out of the bushes, wearing a hooded sweatshirt and carrying the tape and rope he needed for a campaign of terror. Jody, paralyzed with fear when he jumped out at her, tried to run, struggled, screamed. He demanded money. She said she would go home and get some.

Then a three-foot tree limb came crashing down on her face, catching her forehead, her nose, her mouth. She slumped to the tracks and watched blood drip from her face. When he pulled her onto her feet she struggled again, refusing to keep quiet. The only way to keep sane, she recalled later, "was to keep talking and keep hearing myself and make sure I was still there."

The tree limb came down again, smashing into her thigh. He pulled off her sweatshirt, pinned her arms with his knees and covered her mouth, nose, and eyes with tape. He tied her hands behind her back and marched her to a pond in water up to her waist. He pulled her back onto the bank, removed her clothing and raped her.

She asked if he was going to kill her. "Promise you won't," she muttered over and over. His only replies were, "Si, senorita," and "No, senorita." He raped her again. He ran his fingers through her hair and told her she was a great lover.

Jody then heard something that to the rapist may have sounded like a bird in the marsh, but to Jody it signified a miracle: it was a loon call that her boyfriend often used. When she heard the call again, she screamed.

Her attacker left, then came back. He jerked the tape off her face and she saw his angular face, the sunken cheeks, the piercing eyes she had seen before he attacked her—then he left.

Soon her boyfriend was beside her, untying her hands. In the emergency room a police evidence technician took pictures of the rope marks on her wrists, the scrapings on her back, the bruise on her leg, the knob on her nose, her protruding lower lip.

Detective DeRice thought that the rapist might attack again, and he did. He kidnapped and raped a fifteen-year-old girl in nearby Standish. This time he was caught. His name was Larry A. Parks, a thirty-eight-year-old laborer who worked at a construction site near where Jody was raped. He was a federal parolee with a long criminal record. Jody identified him in a police lineup and testified against him before a grand jury and again at the trial. During her testimony she was meticulous, articulate, in control. But as she looked at Parks in the courtroom, she lost it. "It's him, right there," she said, sobbing.

The jury convicted Parks of both attacks and sentenced him to thirty-seven and a half years.

At the time when Jody told her story most rape victims did not want anybody to know what had happened to them. Men were absolved of responsibility by blaming the victim: they were out alone at night, they wore provocative clothing, "they were asking for it." Jody's assailant had none of those excuses. She was proud that Parks was in prison because she endured a year-long legal process, looked him in the eye and identified him as her assailant. She was determined to let women know they could survive a sexual attack.

"I just think of all those women who do nothing," she said. "If I'd done that, this man would still be out there."

The now-defunct Portland *Evening Express* was a small paper, circulation 25,000, in Maine's largest city, population about 70,000. It got a tiny fraction of the attention received by Nancy Ziegenmeyer's story, which was told in Iowa's largest newspaper, then retold in the New York *Times*, and eventually made into a movie. But thousands of Portland residents read an account of a crime whose horror had been shielded from public view before. It was a story writ large by Jody Gould's courage.

When I talked to Jody later, most of her anger toward her attacker was gone. She was sorry he'd had a tough life, but her charity wasn't endless. He had changed her life. She no longer walked with her head in the clouds. She was alert and wary. She carried a billy club when she walked from her car to her house. She didn't walk alone on the beach anymore. Before she took a trip she had her car tuned up and demanded of the mechanic, "Are you positive I'll make it there and back without breaking down?" When she walked on the railroad tracks near the scene of the attack she spewed a stream of obscenities. She heard the cadence of eight sets of male feet turning in the police lineup. But she did not hate men, and she was not ashamed. "I'm alive," she said. "I don't take any of my days for granted."

Because the story was unusual, I asked Jody to come into the newsroom to talk to the staff about it. It was only then that I learned she had agreed to talk to me because I told her I had a daughter her age.

Nothing magically changed after Jody Gould and Nancy Ziegenmeyer told their stories. I would write about sex crimes again later in my career, when I worked for the *Star Tribune* in Minneapolis, where rapists were more likely to be sentenced to two years than 37½. Even today victims' stories are not necessarily believed, nor are their assailants always caught and held accountable. And while victims are treated more humanely now, going through the legal process still can be a horror, and some victims choose not to.

My daughter, Darcy, insisted on telling her story when she was grabbed in a parking garage. She wasn't raped, but her assailant had robbed her of her sense of security in the Maine city where she worked. Because he had committed other, more vicious crimes against other women, she wanted him taken off the street, and she was the only one of his victims capable of showing up for every hearing in his case. She took time off from work and drove an hour to the courthouse each time. Her assailant was found to be mentally ill and hospitalized.

Chapter 19

I was drawn to the issue of drunk driving because of a disturbing inconsistency: We've punished murderers for violating the biblical injunction, "Thou shalt not kill," since the beginning of time, but as a culture we had ignored the tragedy of drunk drivers who kill people just as dead. Historically, they'd been men whose crimes were overlooked in a male-run system in which judges were conditioned to look the other way: "There but for the grace of God go I."

Inspired by the emergence of Mothers Against Drunk Driving, I began to look at these cases in Portland and quickly realized that drunk drivers have stories too. They are often tragic figures addicted to a substance whose addictive qualities weren't recognized for a long time, while their excessive use of alcohol was seen as purely a moral weakness. Either way, they had ruined themselves and their families, as well as the innocents they injured or killed.

In most cases I was drawn to the stories of the victims. But in the case of Robert Lounsbury and Eugene Harley, I was drawn to both. I became aware of the story when I ran into Harley's widow in a courthouse elevator. She showed me a poem Lounsbury had written, expressing grief about his horrendous crime.

Lounsbury grew up in a loving family in Old Town, Maine, "a typical boy," his mother told me, but he was in and out of jail for one offense or another for twenty years. He acknowledged that his family had never deserted him, but he couldn't deny his failures. He failed in the navy and in college. His father, who had given him a job in his mill, kicked him out. He lost a decent job in Florida, selling TV ads, when he slugged a cop, for which he ended up in prison. All of this due to his drinking.

Eugene Harley was an ordinary guy who lived a quiet and productive life. A fisherman and clam digger, he was raised at Cundy's Harbor and was reputed to have the fastest hands in the business for shucking scallops. When he wasn't on the waterfront he worked as a painter. Deserted by his father when he was three, unmarried until he was forty, he was "a very lonesome person until he got married," his wife Helen said.

Helen divorced her previous husband because of alcohol and swore she would never live with a drinker again. "Gene didn't drink that often," she said. But after he drove home from a bar one night they argued about drinking and driving, and he left to live with his mother. Aside from a single chance encounter, she didn't see him again until he was clinging to life in a hospital.

At 4:00 a.m. on an August morning Robert Lounsbury was drag racing on a Portland street when he smashed into Harley's truck. He was so drunk he initially thought someone else was driving, "but all the evidence points to me. They dug me out of the driver's seat. My teeth were on the dashboard."

On the day he was sentenced to seven years in prison, guards took him to Maine Medical Center to see what he had done. Accompanied by a minister who had befriended him in jail, he walked into the room to see Eugene Harley lying on a hospital bed, "a very small form lying on his left side. He was kind of looking at the ceiling 'cause his eyes were open. When you got closer, you could tell there was no awareness behind the eyes."

He saw Helen Harley. "She shows me how they fed him." He heard her say, "I wish you no harm. Just tell the people what alcohol can do."

"Even though I couldn't say anything, I could listen," Lounsbury told me, "and it was more than a surprise that she doesn't hate me."

When I met Lounsbury he was in the Maine State Prison. He was ruggedly good looking, intelligent, articulate, even thoughtful, despite his horrific crime. When Harley died, a year after the crash, he saw himself as a murderer.

How could someone who'd had so much love become a career criminal? His mother wondered, too, thinking maybe they had expected too much of him. Lounsbury had an explanation: he discovered alcohol and sex at the same time in the navy. "Inside of me, even now," he said, "there's a little fat kid, very insecure. There's a lot of why I drink."

The Reverend William Sparks, a minister who worked with and counseled inmates at the Cumberland County Jail, said, yes, Lounsbury came from a stable family, but "failure is comparative. He felt like a failure. He had feelings of not meeting the expectations of others."

In prison Lounsbury worked in the kitchen, making himself healthy food, determined to leave prison in better shape than he came in. He was working toward a college degree in counseling so he could help others, assuage his guilt and, perhaps, keep himself sober. If he were to leave prison that day, I asked him, would he head for the nearest bar? "Ever since this happened, I've wondered if I'll drink again," he replied. "I'm inclined to say yes. If I could take odds, I'd go with the drink instead of the abstinence."

In saying that Lounsbury was being "dangerously honest" at his own expense, Sparks said. He believed Lounsbury had the will and the ability to stay sober.

A week after Eugene Harley died, Helen went out in a friend's lobster boat and scattered her husband's ashes in Cundy's Harbor. "He'll be at peace there," she said. "He'll be with the sea that he loved. He'll be close to the people he was born and brought up with. He's a free person like he was when I first met him."

I pursued this issue through the years as awareness grew, sentences became longer and fewer people drove drunk. Still, nearly thirty people a day—one every fifty minutes—die in drunk driving crashes. The yearly number of deaths have fallen over three decades, but drunk driving still claims more than 10,000 lives a year. And many victims' stories die with them.

38. When Jody told her story, most rape victims didn't want anyone to know what happened to them. But Laura was proud that Larry A. Parks went to prison because she endured a year-long legal process, looked him in the eye and identified him as her assailant. She wanted women to know they could survive a sexual attack.

39. "Even though I couldn't say anything, I could listen," Robert Lounsbury told me, "and it was more than a surprise that she doesn't hate me." When I met Lounsbury he was in the Maine State Prison. He was ruggedly good looking, intelligent, articulate, even thoughtful, despite his horrific crime. When Harley died, a year after the crash, he saw himself as a murderer.

Chapter 20

"O, oh, here comes the First Amendment!" Assistant U.S. Attorney Bill Browder would say as I walked into the federal courthouse. That comment makes me smile even today.

Portland, a small city, is Maine's legal and economic hub, with more lawyers per capita than Washington, DC, and a federal court that engaged me and tested my reporting skills. I was a rather earnest reporter, taking my First Amendment rights seriously. There were untold stories here, and I was free to pursue them.

One story, especially misery ridden, begged to be told. Despite the deadly impact of asbestos on Maine shipyard workers and others worldwide, that story had languished for years. By the time I arrived in Portland asbestos accounted for a third of the cases in U.S. District Court for Maine. The state had a shipbuilding history going back four hundred years, and it became one of the most dangerous industries for exposure to asbestos. With two big shipyards located in the state, more than four hundred shipyard workers died of mesothelioma and other asbestos-related diseases between 1999 and 2013. A so-called miracle insulating material, asbestos is a naturally occurring mineral that, because it is strong, lightweight, won't burn or transmit heat, and resists corrosion by chemicals, it is contained in more than six thousand products. The ancient Greeks and Romans knew about it.

For years the asbestos industry had worked to bury these cases, settling out of court or in other ways keeping them from coming to trial. They involved the classic question that would become part of nearly every products liability case before long: What did the asbestos industry know, and when did they know it? It turned out they knew in the late 1930s that inhaling asbestos fibers was hazardous to health. That was why it seemed to me to be so important to write about them.

In the courtroom the issues seemed esoteric, involving an ever-thickening web of legal theories, but it really was a tragedy—the story of a worldwide industry built on a lucrative but deadly substance that struck down millions of workers in their prime, but was ignored for decades in order to protect profits. Because it presented important legal and public health issues I covered it throughout my time in Portland. As with everything else, I learned on the job. I covered so many hearings on the topic that Judge Edward T. Gignoux jokingly asked me after one hearing if I wanted to write his ruling.

The case of Blaine and Margaret Austin v. Bath Iron Works, the first to come to trial in Maine, became a symposium on the deadly effects of asbestos and responsibility for those effects. Bath Iron Works (BIW) was founded in Bath, Maine, in 1884; it makes ships for the U.S. Navy to this day. Austin worked there for twenty-four years, painting hot and cold-water pipes on ships and cleaning up asbestos dust and scraps after other workers had insulated the pipes.

In 1971 the U. S. Department of Labor ordered a reduction in the number of fibers workers could be exposed to. In 1972 it lowered the level still further but delayed implementation until 1976. By then Blaine Austin was already sick.

In 1978 the U.S. Department of Health, Education, and Welfare warned of the dangers of inhaling asbestos dust and fibers. By then Blaine Austin was dead. He died an agonizing death from mesothelioma, an always fatal cancer of the chest cavity, on October 13, 1977, a day after his forty-sixth birthday.

It was undisputed at trial that asbestos manufacturers had known for decades that asbestos was dangerous. Their own records showed that knowledge convincingly. As a result, most of the sixteen companies sued by Margaret Austin settled with her before trial for a bare bones total of $275,000. The two holdouts blamed BIW for failing to protect its workers, but because the shipyard provided workers' compensation for injuries, it could not be held accountable.

The jury found the companies negligent but said Blaine Austin was also negligent for failing to protect his own health, mainly by not always wearing a respirator, which was hot and uncomfortable. Austin's attorneys were shocked by the finding. So was Margaret Austin, who said her husband was a careful man who threw away his cigarettes the instant he heard the surgeon general's warning about smoking.

Although she lost, she eventually got a new trial because of a change in the law. The new jury ruled for Austin and awarded her $323,456 in a wrongful death verdict.

Maine has the highest death rate from asbestos-caused disease in the nation. According to the Environmental Working Group, from 1999 to 2013, 2003 Maine people died from asbestos exposure. Nearly four decades after I first covered this litigation, it continues around the country, as more than 12,000 people die from asbestos disease each year. Although the mineral is now regulated, it continues to turn up in consumer products, including crayons imported from China and cosmetics marketed to young girls.

§

When the Coast Guard began intercepting marijuana smuggling boats off the coast of Florida in the 1970s, resourceful smugglers moved their operations into the nooks and crannies of the Maine coast. But the Coast Guard got wise to these operations too, and they were able to intercept some (probably small) percentage of the smuggling operations. Some of these cases brought high drama to Portland's federal court, and not a small amount of interest from the reading public.

One of these high-profile cases I liked to call the Case of Cannabis and Coptics. Members of the Ethiopian Zion Coptic Church, based in Miami and Jamaica, were caught with twenty-one tons of marijuana off the coast of Maine. They claimed they smuggled all of that marijuana into Maine for their personal use. Perhaps they thought that this case would be a breeze—that they would end up before a lackadaisical judge in a sleepy backwater. But Judge Edward T. Gignoux, one of the most revered judges in Maine history and a finalist for the U.S. Supreme Court, ran his courtroom with awesome authority. An attorney for one drug smuggler said of him, "He was one of the greatest judges I ever appeared before."

Long-haired and bearded, the smugglers came into court wearing colorful church sashes, and smoked marijuana on the courthouse steps during breaks. Judge Gignoux was livid when he found out about it. He told them that if they did that again they would go to jail for the duration of the trial. No doubt their lawyers told them this was one judge they should not mess with. The pot smoking stopped (at least in plain sight), and in the end all but one of the fifteen defendants were convicted.

§

The second case, which had more literary than religious overtones, we can call the Case of Richard Stratton and His Friend Norman Mailer. Stratton was thirty-seven when he was accused of smuggling thirty tons of marijuana into Maine. In his defense he claimed that he consorted with smugglers in order to write a book about the drug trade, but never joined their conspiracies.

The case generated a lot of buzz when Stratton's influential friends Norman Mailer and popular historian Doris Kearns Goodwin came to testify on his behalf. Mailer and Stratton owned a horse farm together in Phillips, Maine, and Doris Kearns Goodwin had a summer home nearby. Kearns Goodwin, who won a Pulitzer Prize for her book about Franklin and Eleanor Roosevelt, testified that Stratton was obsessed with the drug world, but she did not know if he had crossed the line from research into smuggling. Mailer was never able to take the stand because Judge Gignoux would not allow him to testify out of turn. But he told me in a street interview that Stratton was "the kind of fellow who would run up five stories in a burning tenement to get your children out."

Norman Mailer was charming. He gave me his home phone number—I kept it a long time, like a 1950s kid with a Willie Mays autograph—and he remembered my name when I saw him a second time weeks later. He said he had delivered Stratton's book to a New York literary agent, who told him it "was not a great work of art but has large commercial possibilities."

I was dubious. Stratton gave me a draft, a thick sheaf of papers that was mostly quotations with little plot. A jury convicted Stratton. Judge Gignoux sentenced him to 25 years, which Stratton, using legal skills acquired in his own case, got reduced to eight. He eventually settled in New York City and has had a successful career as a writer and producer of books, feature films, and documentaries.

When his memoir, "Smuggler's Blues: A True Story of the Hippie Mafia," was published in 2016, he stated in an online interview that prosecutors had offered to drop the charges against him if he would inform on Mailer. For what, I don't know, but Stratton refused, saying Mailer was an innocent bystander. A member of an old New England family, he told an interviewer that he became "an adrenaline junkie" while smuggling drugs from Mexico as a college student in Arizona. "Getting in a big load, getting one over on law enforcement, the rush from that, I became addicted to that rush," he said.

40. Me with Judge Edward T. Gignoux, one of the most revered judges in Maine history and a finalist for the U.S. Supreme Court. He ran his courtroom with awesome authority. An attorney for a drug smuggler once said of him, "He was one of the greatest judges I ever appeared before."

Chapter 21

D readlocked Rastafarians and hippie outlaws made for good copy and exciting days in the federal courthouse, but the most compelling and significant drug smuggling case I covered in Portland was the case of Michael Tindall. Tindall was a patriot. He should have been a hero. He grew up on a farm outside Princeton, New Jersey, a college town where Vietnam protests were endemic. But he was not a privileged college kid; he was a high school graduate in a middleclass family, and he felt an obligation to serve his country. At nineteen he enlisted.

Tindall trained to become a helicopter pilot and was deployed for a year-long tour of duty in Vietnam in April of 1970. He flew 755 combat hours in helicopter gunships, earning a Distinguished Flying Cross, thirty-two air medals, and two bronze stars. But he returned home not as a hero but as a castaway from an unpopular war. Rejected for pilots' jobs when he returned, he created a war-like milieu around himself, engaging in every dangerous activity he could find. He found meaning in smuggling drugs to recreate the danger of his wartime flying missions.

Tindall was accused of smuggling thirty tons of marijuana with a street value of $36 million into an old fish factory in an isolated Maine cove. By the time the feds found out about it the marijuana was long gone, but Tindall and others were arrested after a fellow Vietnam vet snitched on them.

In the 1980 trial in Portland's federal court, his Boston attorney, James Lawson, told the jury that Tindall saw more combat duty "than almost any soldier who fought in Vietnam" and he "came back from that horror legally insane." Lawson told me, "I always understood this was a new and novel defense. Whether twelve people would find him not guilty because the Vietnam war had made him crazy was always a worrying proposition. But the facts were true, and the arguments were fair and just."

The defense seemed more suited to cases of veterans who committed crimes in outbursts of rage. There had been few *nonviolent* post-traumatic stress disorder (PTSD) cases like this one, but Tindall was acquitted six years earlier in a Massachusetts hashish smuggling case using that defense. John P. Wilson, an Ohio psychologist who was the leading authority on the readjustment problems of Vietnam veterans, testified that Tindall had the second or third worst case of PTSD among 3,000 veterans he had interviewed. This was an emerging defense, often called the "Vietnam syndrome," that the government fiercely resisted.

When the trial opened Assistant U.S. Attorney Jay McCloskey laid out the complicated nature of smuggling cases and the elaborate planning they required. He argued that Tindall knew what he was doing but chose not to conform his conduct to the requirements of the law.

The jury—and the lucky journalists who got to cover the trial—saw the best of two whip-smart young lawyers: McCloskey, a self-described "Bangor boy," who graduated from the University of Maine and its law school, and later would become U.S. attorney for Maine; versus Lawson, a Texan whose drawl survived his Ivy League education at Harvard, a detour to Harvard Divinity School, and law school at Boston College. He would spend all of his working life as a defense attorney.

The defense Lawson laid before the jury might have caused many judges to ask, "Is this a real defense?" Especially Judge Edward T. Gignoux, who always had an eye out for nonsense. But, Lawson said, "Judge Gignoux was fairly convinced after hearing the testimony that Mike Tindall had suffered a lot, and there were reasons behind what he did."

"He made great contributions to his country in a war that affected him deeply, and he was treated badly when he returned," Lawson said of Tindall. "He told me, 'When I came home, the liberals hated me because I went. The conservatives hated me because we lost.'"

Judge Gignoux may have been impressed by the letters that Tindall's mother read to the jury. In the first, he told her not to worry, that he had decent food, a nice place to live, and was safe.

In the last he wrote that he was "killing gooks every day and having a very nice time."

Tindall himself did not testify, so little of his personal story came out in the trial. But I learned that story in the courthouse hallway, listening to him for four hours while we awaited the verdict. With deep lines etched in his thirty-two-year-old face, he was handsome, articulate, and a deliberate speaker, allowing me to take down nearly every word in longhand. He did not want me to use a tape recorder.

His story was different from many other Vietnam veterans, most of whom were drafted. While others evaded the draft by fleeing to Canada, deliberately injuring themselves, or altering doctors' certificates, Tindall enlisted. I knew one draft-age young man who had his wife drive over his arm with his car. It didn't work: he was drafted and ended up with a cushy job (not available to poor or black draftees) driving generals around in Texas. I knew another young man who was called back for a physical because his paperwork had been lost; he saw the same doctor he'd seen before. "What did I say before?" the doc asked. "You failed me," he replied. He escaped the draft. Tindall's patriotism made him different.

As a teenager, Tindall said, "I couldn't say it was an immoral war because I didn't know whether it was moral. The people who were running the country said it was. Surely, they were more qualified to make that decision than I was, sitting in New Jersey at seventeen years old."

It was the spring of 1970. Tindall was twenty years old when he was sent to Vietnam. In a photo he looked eerily like one of the handsome British poets who became famous while fighting in World War I.

Tindall loved the idea of flying and worked at an airport after high school before enlisting. Having volunteered to fly gunships, Tindall found himself leading a two-helicopter team with incredible destructive capacity. Each copter carried 38 17-pound rockets, each with the power of a 105 mm howitzer cannon; two GE mini-guns capable of firing 4,000 rounds a minute; an M-5 grenade launcher that could fire 240 grenades a minute; and M-60 machine guns capable of firing 720 rounds a minute.

He ended up in Binh Dinh Province as a member of the 129th Assault Helicopter Company, in a unit called the Cobras, a close-knit group who flew over Vietnam villages they had just destroyed dropping "calling cards" that said, "Call us for death and destruction day or night. You call, we kill."

Despite the awesome firepower, Tindall soon came to believe the war could not be won. It followed that Vietnam was the wrong place for him—and his government—to be. By fighting an enemy that could effectively camouflage itself, "you had to kill civilians," he said. And by killing civilians, "you were recruiting more Viet Cong and VC sympathy than you were eliminating."

Not long after arriving in the country Tindall was directed to fly into Cambodia on a combat mission. He returned from that mission to hear President Richard Nixon say over armed services television that the United States had no intention of violating Cambodia's sovereign territory.

No longer believing in the war, Tindall developed what he says was the only possible rationale for continuing to fight: "The more enemy we could kill, the more of our kids, sent there by a criminally negligent government, would be able to go home."

"There were atrocities committed that no one who wasn't there could ever understand—not Korean vets, not World War II vets, and not World War I vets," he said. But, he added, "it was not the horrors of war that did it. It's the rage that you felt at knowing that your own government murdered those kids. They died because Vietnam was a bad war. They died because the people who ran our government and military were making totally self-centered, treasonous decisions to continue the fighting until they could fool us into thinking we had not lost our first war in history, and that we did indeed need to be there."

The Cobras developed an esprit de corps and a razor-sharp alertness to survive: "We would risk our lives at the drop of a hat to save one other person."

"When you're flying a gunship, if you become apprehensive or scared or want to go home, if you lost the commitment to killing anything under you, you lost the razor's edge that kept you alive. You had to have no second thoughts whatsoever. You had to build walls in your mind to shut out any type of emotion other than aggression. We used the slogan, 'Yea, though I walk through the valley of the shadow of death, I shall fear no evil, because I am the evilest bastard in the valley.' That's the attitude we needed to stay alive and be aggressive, effective attack helicopter pilots."

At night they numbed themselves on marijuana, having quit alcohol because it gave them hangovers. Marijuana "was unofficially condoned," Tindall said. He recalled a flight surgeon lecturing pilots on the dangers of various drugs and saying, "Everybody needs something to relax over here. I'm not a pilot, but if I was, I know the alternative I'd choose."

"I'm not saying marijuana is good for you," Tindall said, "I knew at the time, though, that in that situation it was the most effective and benign substance that I could use to allow me to maintain what little sanity I had left, and safeguard my crew and my mission."

When he first heard about the case, his attorney, James Lawson, was not prepared to be sympathetic to Tindall and the Vietnam buddies who came to Portland to support him. A self-described "long-haired hippie" at Harvard, he had been against the war, "but I fell in love with his story because it was so compelling. It broke my heart. It was hard not to hear that story of very patriotic, very decent, lower middleclass kids who went off to do what their government asked them to do and came back damaged goods. These guys were so young. They were asked to do terrible things. I think they were fairly desperate for their story to be told."

Tindall's story after he returned from Vietnam included 115 job rejections in two years. The rejection spiral was broken when Air America offered him a job ferrying a Canadian peace-keeping team around Southeast Asia. But then the Viet Cong swept through South Vietnam, shattering a fragile truce and taking Tindall's job with them.

Back in the U.S., Tindall got a call from Peter Krutschewski, his former commander, who said he was doing "some dangerous and exciting flying," and invited Tindall to join him. He replied, "I'll be there in the morning."

Thus began Mexican marijuana smuggling ventures involving, among others, Tindall, Krutschewski, and Ricki Lee Benedict, another member of the Cobras. It was followed by other ventures in Massachusetts and Maine. "If they say in this case that I appreciated the wrongfulness of my conduct in breaking the law, no, I did not. Because to me [marijuana] had the same effect it had in Vietnam," Tindall said. "It helped push the tidal waves of emotion out of my head. It was a dam, a buffer. I wanted a mission again … I'd say they were probably the most dangerous missions I ever flew in my life. You had to fly so low, with no lights on, through mountains and deserts, landing on roads and deserts in the middle of the night."

He was glad Krutschewski had called "because I don't know what would have happened if I'd let this fester in that apartment for a few more days. But I know it would have been more destructive to myself, and maybe some innocent people, than what happened."

Eventually he and his Vietnam buddies got out of smuggling within months of each other. "We quit because we had all started to readjust again," he said. "I started getting uncomfortable feelings about what I was doing. It suddenly dawned on me that if I kept up this insane madness—the ultimate shaft would have been if I killed myself doing these things just trying to get these intrusive thoughts out of my head. If I killed myself, that would be the ultimate victory for the government."

When he arrived in Portland for trial, Tindall was married to his high school sweetheart and had two boys, ages five and four. When his first son was born, "something real strange happened in that delivery room," he said. "It ripped down the concrete walls that were hiding some of my emotions. My ability to cry was reborn with the birth of my boy."

"It was like the poison was draining out of him," his father, Albert, said during the Massachusetts trial.

Then along came Robert Rankin, one of the operatives in the smuggling operation. Rankin was a Vietnam vet who was despised by the others because his military job was burying the dead, and because, they said, his lazy postwar lifestyle was supported by a well-off family. When Rankin was arrested he copped a deal, fingering dozens of people from his own smuggling ventures. Tindall was one of them, along with his compatriots in the Massachusetts and Maine cases. "That indictment was not brought down on me," Tindall said. "It was brought down on a person who no longer existed."

Among the Vietnam brothers who came to Portland to support him, one had taken out a second mortgage on his house to be there. The Cobra crews had an intense bond, backed by a code that exemplified their horrible missions: kill everybody in sight, take no prisoners, strafe villages without mercy, defoliate the countryside. The code words were "Go hot."

Lawson was about to begin his closing arguments when he heard a rustle in the courtroom as one of the veterans left his seat and approached him with a note. "I opened it up and it said, 'Go hot,'" Lawson told me. "It was maybe the most important thing that happened to me in that case."

After all the drama and brilliant argumentation, the jury could not decide whether Tindall was guilty or not. A hung jury was declared and a second trial was scheduled. Michael Tindall was convicted in the second trial in 1982, but because of the severity of his war-induced illness, Judge Gignoux sentenced him to only two years.

Following this surprisingly successful outcome lawyers called James Lawson from all over the country seeking help with cases involving Vietnam vets. Psychologist John Wilson began to do even more work with veterans suffering from PTSD.

Lawson said he kept in touch with Michael Tindall for a long time. "He was glad that somebody stood up for him and let his story be heard. I'm very fond of him."

41. Attorney James Lawson. Following the surprisingly successful outcome of the Michael Tindall trial, lawyers called Lawson from all over the country seeking help with cases involving Vietnam veterans. Lawson said of Tindall, "He was glad that somebody stood up for him and let his story be heard. I'm very fond of him."

42. Judge Jim Watson grew up in Harlem and was seriously injured as an infantryman in World War II. He said he would not join his friends in the Freedom Rides: "The days of somebody beating up on me are over.

Chapter 22

T he most significant civil trial I covered in Maine was the case of Joe Ricci v. Key Bank, which produced the largest jury award in Maine history. It also brought to Portland the most amazing judge I'd ever seen in action, whose likes I would never see again.

Joe Ricci was a troubled-kid-turned-successful-businessman who owned a Maine racetrack and a school for troubled kids. Ricci and his partner, psychiatrist Gerald E. Davidson, sued Key Bank after it cut off their $1 million line of credit based on erroneous information that Ricci had ties to organized crime.

Jim Watson was an esteemed judge from a well-known New York family with Jamaican roots and stellar accomplishments. A judge on the U.S. Court of International Trade, Watson was called in to handle the case because of its potentially explosive nature and Ricci's mercurial temperament. Watson's family included Colin Powell, a cousin who became U.S. Secretary of State. His father was the first black judge in New York state. Martin Luther King was a family friend. Adam Clayton Powell taught him to fish. He shot pool with Willie Mays. When John F. Kennedy was running for president, he called in Watson to get advice on how to deal with minorities. "John Kennedy didn't have a clue about Black people," he told me.

He grew up in Harlem and was seriously injured in World War II while serving in the all-black 371st Regiment, 92nd Division. Though he was vice president of the New York City NAACP in the 1960s, he would not join his black friends protesting segregation in the Freedom Rides. "I said, 'No way. I have been trained to be violent. The days of somebody beating up on me are over. I was an infantryman. I would not do the movement any good because the first time [someone got violent with me] I would respond.'"

Watson met Vice President Lyndon Baines Johnson in 1962 when President Kennedy appointed him as a member of the U.S. delegation, headed by Johnson, to the Jamaican independence celebration. The two men and their wives became friends. When Johnson became president he nominated Watson to the U.S. Customs Court, but the nomination was caught in the crossfire between Johnson and then New York Senator Robert Kennedy, who detested each other. One day Kennedy gave up his misgivings and called Watson in. "He said, 'Judge, I don't know you.' I said, 'With all due respect, Senator, that is not my problem. I have lived in New York all my life.'" That was a jab at Kennedy, whose famous family was deeply ensconced in Massachusetts; he was perceived as a carpetbagger when he was elected to the Senate from New York.

Watson left the meeting with Kennedy's approval, but with misgivings about being appointed to an obscure court. "This is like being sworn into retirement," he told himself. "This court has none of the pit work that you do in District Court." But he decided that the court, later renamed the U.S. Court of International Trade, did important work, so he took the job. He discovered that he could still find "pit work" in District Courts around the country, including Portland, when judges were needed.

Ordinarily, I was the only reporter covering the federal court, but this trial was a big deal and it drew a slew of media. Because of my hearing problem, I had established a special place in the courtroom where I had a straight-on view of the witness box. That way I could read lips. When an artist asked if she could sit there during the Ricci trial, I said no. This was the only way I could do my work.

The bank and its holding company had several lawyers, including Thomas Burns of Boston, a small man who sat on a big pile of money: he had three homes listed in the phone book. Each day as I entered the courtroom, Burns attacked me for that morning's story, and the complaint was always the same—my coverage was slanted to the prosecution's side. I carried his complaints to my editors, who invariably found no merit in them. I wasn't going to defend myself to him—it wasn't my style, and I would never confront an attorney in the middle of a trial. But I did get sick of his complaining, so I started coming in a tiny bit late. Nobody took my seat. I was in that spot every day for seven weeks.

When Judge Watson sent the jury to deliberate it was evident by Burns' struts, his smirks, his pumped-out chest that he thought he had won. When the jury returned after 17½ hours of deliberation over three days, it awarded Ricci and Davidson $15 million. The jury decided that Key Bank had violated its contract with Ricci and Davidson to act fairly and in good faith, and it had intentionally inflicted emotional distress on Ricci.

Burns had been confident that the bank had won, that he had won. He was sure that Ricci and Davidson would get nothing. I thought the jury would award them $10 million but kept that to myself. The next day the jury awarded $12.5 million more in punitive damages. The last time I saw Burns he was looking out a courthouse window quoting the poem "If—" by Rudyard Kipling: "If you can keep your head when all about you / Are losing theirs and blaming it on you ..."

Judge Watson threw out the punitive damages, and Key Bank settled with Ricci and Davidson for $10 million to avoid an expensive appeal.

"I think the people of Maine made a statement about rights," Ricci said afterward. "As Judge Watson said, 'As Maine goes, so goes the nation.'"

For the spectators who came back day after day, the verdict was anticlimactic, but they had seen a good show. Watson's legal brilliance was evident even to non-lawyers, and he channeled it with charm and humor. It plainly was not legal artifice, but who he was. He called frequent breaks, with explanatory labels for each type— CRFB (court reporter's finger break) in honor of "stenographic pianist" Harry Hagopian; WNB (Watson nicotine break) for a habit the judge said he could not break; and SRBB (Shirley Richardson birthday break) in honor of a juror.

When Burns demanded that the judge "chastise" Bob Axelrod, Ricci's attorney, for something he had done, Watson broke up the courtroom by giving Axelrod a shame-on-you gesture, rubbing one index finger over the other. When I wrote a story about him mid-trial he said, "I was trying to be incognegro." When one attorney objected to another attorney's questioning, he said, "Objection sustained. And don't wake me up again."

Dave Astor, a 1960s Portland television personality, was in the courtroom daily while awaiting hip surgery. Like Watson, he was in his sixties, a World War II veteran, and gregarious. One day Watson called him into his chambers and the two became friends. "When you're in his presence, there's the feeling that you're in the presence of greatness," Astor said. "You know there's something very special there, but he never imposed that."

One day the bailiff called me in during a break. This was Astor's doing, "You have to meet Donna." It felt uncomfortable for a journalist to go into the judge's chambers in the middle of a trial, but such was Watson's presence that my body followed my feet into his chambers. He was talking on the phone, and he handed the phone to me, saying, "Here, talk to my wife." I didn't know what to say, but DiJaris Watson seemed accustomed to talking to strangers at her husband's behest. She was an accomplished person in her own right, having worked for two presidents and three New York City mayors, and she was gracious.

"We found that he could be like us, that he was approachable," Astor said. "When he was on the bench he was as good a judge as can be, and once he took the robes off, he was a really nice guy and a pal." After the trial, Watson wrote to Astor, "So it ends, seven weeks of toil and turmoil, sweetened by the remembrance and the pleasure of your company during this period."

Years later, after Watson's wife died and I had moved to Minnesota, he called me from time to time. He called Dave Astor too. He loved to talk on the phone, and he was lonely. We were a reminder of the special time we had shared in the Portland pit.

Chapter 23

I asked Managing Editor Steve Riley if the newspaper would help me pay for hearing aids, and I submitted an audiologist's report to human resources showing my hearing loss to be moderate to severe. Riley responded with a deep-throated "Are you kidding?" laugh. Human resources didn't respond.

When I was trying to enter the newspaper profession in the 1960s I quickly realized that I had a major disability: gender. I knew I had another disability, hearing loss, but I decided to keep that one to myself. After all, I had worked my way through college and received a journalism degree with honors in spite of it.

In my college days, when I went to the University of Minnesota health service to have my ears unplugged, the doctor asked if I'd ever considered hearing aids. I said no, and I agreed to try them. He put generic hearing aids in my ears and sent me off to the noisiest place on campus, the cafeteria in the student union. The clatter of plates and the clamor of voices made me realize there were some things I did not want to hear. "Why did he do that?" I asked myself years later. Surely he knew that's what would happen. It's as if he was saying, "There are worse things than not being able to hear. Stop feeling sorry for yourself." That put off any consideration of hearing aids until I was in my thirties.

When I look back, it seems like the 1950s and 1960s were still the dark ages for people with disabilities. Historically, people who couldn't hear, like people who couldn't see, were cared for by their families, reflecting a view that these were individual failings, not society's problems. Our hearing loss wasn't even fully understood by our families, who obviously could not know what we were not hearing. We coped as best we could.

I didn't mention my hearing problem on my first job in Albany. For a long time, I didn't mention it in Portland either. I wasn't going to say, "You'd better find someone else to cover the courts because I don't hear very well." That was a plum job and I wanted it! Now I was a successful and valued reporter. I had won awards. Editor John Murphy sent me a note saying, "When I count my blessings, I count you." I thought it was reasonable to ask for an accommodation that would help me do my job as the paper's court reporter. But apparently Riley and the human resources director didn't see it that way. The dark ages still existed.

So I went back to the skills I'd developed as a seven-year-old, when my parents had my tonsils and adenoids removed—intense concentration, lip reading, sitting up front, and not being afraid to ask questions when I needed to.

As a child I found comfort in solitude, and social connections in books. Sometimes I just tuned out. As a child my hearing problem truly was a deep, dark secret. A few years ago Pat Olson Schultz, one of my best friends from Peterson, told me that she never knew that I was hearing impaired. "You must have been reading my lips, and I didn't even know it," she said. "That's how good you were."

I was stunned. Surely I must have told someone. But I didn't. Why would I? Since age seven I had carried around the idea that there was something wrong with me, it was shameful, it was probably my fault, and it was my job to fix it. I don't know where I got the outrageous idea that I could become a journalist.

I covered the courts in Portland for eight years, and later, in Minneapolis, I was the *Star Tribune*'s legal affairs reporter for six years. It was always a struggle, but with the coping mechanisms I had developed, I succeeded, and the truth is, I made few errors in my thirty-two years of reporting because I worked so hard at hearing. In Portland, I bought my first hearing aids, but there was so much background noise that they weren't useful, and I ditched them.

In Minneapolis I acquired better hearing aids, but I had to turn them up so high to hear witnesses that they made me nauseous. That's when I decided I couldn't be in courtrooms anymore and took on a newly created consumer reporting beat. I had a special device to help me hear on the phone, and I used email and the internet as often as possible to conduct interviews and gather information.

The Portland *Press Herald* had shrugged off my problem, and I never told my *Star Tribune* bosses I had trouble hearing. Until the day I retired it was a silent disability. Reporting on the law was the joy of my working life but I had to let it go.

§

The idea of hearing as a "silent disability" came to me in the story I wrote of five suburban Minneapolis women in their seventies who had hearing problems. They met regularly for the camaraderie and social acceptance they couldn't get in the hearing world. They were physically active, mentally sharp, and willing to tell jokes on themselves, but life was hard. Even though they all wore hearing aids, they might not speak at events or meetings, or they might bluff their way through, wondering afterward if they had said something inappropriate. "You nod a lot," said one. "You feel dumb, really dumb," said another. These women were too scrappy to give up on life, but they knew others who withdrew because coping in the outside world was too difficult.

When they decided to go public with a program they had started at a women's club called the Hearing M'aids, I realized the story of hearing loss was ripe for telling. This story generated as much response as any non-investigative piece I wrote in my seventeen years at the *Star Tribune*. After it went national, emails and phone calls streamed in from all over the country, showing how pervasive, debilitating, and often lonely hearing loss can be.

One woman commended me for writing about "a disability that no one talks about. Someone who loses their hearing often becomes isolated and depressed and needs to know there are many others who have this same disability."

A ninety-year-old woman wrote, "I have family members who talk to me from the other room with their heads in the closet." And an Arizona man said, "I have asked people to speak slower and more distinctly so I can hear what they say, but it lasts about three sentences."

A twenty-two-year-old said she identified with the women even though they were much older: "The nod that you give someone you can't hear, the embarrassment you feel all the way to your gut, the simple envy of people who can hear."

Of course the story of the Hearing M'aids was my story, too. But I didn't acknowledge my complicity in it when I wrote the piece. I decided not to reveal that I too was hearing impaired. In retrospect, I think that perhaps readers had a right to know. But my reluctance to reveal that this was my story too is just another example of the shame of the silent disability.

Chapter 24

I see my husband striding down the sidewalk outside our Portland workplace. He is back from his doctor's appointment, and he's smiling. Good news, I think. Then he says shocking words, "I have cancer."

Cancer? My thirty-eight-year-old husband has cancer? My husband, who doesn't even catch colds?

I open my mouth to speak, but no words come out. I try to walk toward Jon, but my feet feel glued to the sidewalk.

I need to know the details, but the details make it worse. This is not just cancer but one of the really bad ones, multiple myeloma, which, at the time, was usually fatal in two years. It's Thursday. Chemotherapy starts Monday. The Portland doctor—we'll call him Dr. Holland—didn't give us a chance to get a second opinion. In our shock, we didn't even think about that.

It doesn't make sense that Jon has this cancer, nor does it make sense that life goes on. Later, it seems as though a cocoon has spun itself around our heads that lets us see, hear, and breathe, but shuts off our brains' emotional sensors. As days go by the strands of the cocoon unwind, and we have to deal with it.

We try to paper over the "I have cancer" words with ordinary conversation, then "two years" jumps in. Medical literature gave patients two years, but Dr. Holland said he and other myeloma specialists around the country were getting better results. He gives Jon six to twelve years. Should we feel good about that? In our emotional stupor we do feel good about that. Later, we realize what the doctor didn't say, "Oh, by the way, you're going to die from this disease. No one survives it."

The chemotherapy schedule is three days a week for two weeks, then two weeks off. Each time, Jon comes home and goes to bed, waiting for the chills, fever, and headache that always descend on him. I smother him in blankets when he is cold, put cold cloths on his head when he is hot. Finally he sleeps, and I sleep, too. The next day we go to work. This goes on for six months.

I am thirty-nine and I consider myself pretty tough, but nothing in my life experience has prepared me for this. What do we do? How do we do it? I'm not focusing on making the best of Jon's remaining days. No, it's not that at all. I will chase the cancer away. I will make him salads every day, my whacked-out brain says. But six to twelve years keep staring at me, a ghostly presence.

About this time—it was 1984—a reign of terror began in the Portland newsroom, originated by an editor who had arrived as a reporter ten years earlier and had been climbing the ladder ever since. He had already hired ten or so young staffers, but in an economic downtown shortly afterward, he had to fire all of them.

Then he decided to remake the newsroom by getting rid of seasoned hands, no doubt to replace us with young loyalists. This was traumatic for the hard-working, capable older reporters and editors who had kept the place going in difficult times. Two who were fired never regained the income they lost.

Jon and I found ourselves in the middle of the morass. When Jon, the editor of the entertainment section, was required to document every twenty minutes of his time, and I, the court reporter, was not allowed to go to the courthouses without permission, we knew the end was near. We had wanted to spend our lives in Maine, but we knew that this toxic atmosphere could not be good for Jon's health. We made the only decision that made sense: returning to our native Minnesota.

When we weren't able to get jobs from afar, Jon, an Anglophile, said, "Maybe we should quit our jobs and go to England for a while." He expected me, the keeper of our finances, to say, "Are you crazy?" I said, "Great! Let's do it."

We sold our house, found a sitter for Barney, our beagle, and settled Darcy, who was now twenty-one years old, into an apartment. Although she was now a young adult, as an only child she wasn't really ready to fend for herself with a father far away, dying of cancer. She felt abandoned, and it affected her for years to come. We selfishly focused on ourselves and later regretted it mightily.

The trip to Ireland and England gave us the respite we needed, but it had a hard edge. We were living with a deadly cancer. We had left our suffering daughter behind. We had no home or jobs to go back to when we returned. The only good news was that we had money from an inflated housing market to live on.

The highlight of our time away was seeing twenty plays. One was "The Life and Death of King John," one of Shakespeare's lesser-known plays. At the end of the performance an actor came on the stage to tell us that an ancient Shakespeare theater had been discovered on the banks of the Thames, and that a development company was going to raze it to construct an office building. He invited us to go to the site the next day to join actors in a protest.

We went the next day and saw some of the best-known actors of the London stage reading Shakespeare on the sidewalk. One was a strikingly handsome actor, in his midtwenties, not yet famous but he would become so: Ralph Fiennes. "Schindler's List" was still off on the horizon, along with other movies for which he would receive rave reviews. With my zoom lens I photographed him, and he didn't seem to mind. When he seemed to be looking for a tool to open his beer, I dug one out of my purse. I was always a well-stocked traveler. He asked if I would be coming back. I said I wouldn't, but I couldn't help but flutter my brown eyes at his baby blues.

Many of the actors would be staying there overnight, and I wanted to join them, but I had been ill in Ireland and couldn't risk being out in the chilly night air. Plus, the trains were going to be on strike the next day.

§

When we returned to Minnesota in the summer of 1989, we barely recognized the Twin Cities we had left twenty-one years earlier—it was much too big for us and fiendishly hot. We thought we'd made a mistake, but within three months we both had jobs, Jon as Managing Editor of the alumni magazine at Macalester College, me as a reporter for the *Star Tribune*.

Since chemotherapy ended, Jon had felt fine. His new doctor told him that if he had walked in off the street she would have a hard time diagnosing him with the disease. On another visit she told him he had "a durable, long-term, partial remission." Did he no longer have a terminal illness? "That's what I would say," she said. The Maine doctor, with his estimate of six to twelve years, had been optimistic, she said, because the median survival time for patients of all ages was three years.

Jon's next doctor said he didn't think Jon ever had cancer! There was no indication in Jon's medical records from 1984—ten years earlier—that he did. And if he did, he wouldn't have lived more than four years. He suggested the diagnosing doctor "was committed to a pathway he couldn't get out of ... We all make mistakes. I've made mistakes." But he had other concerns about Dr. Holland's care. He said it was dangerous to remove bone marrow from the sternum as Holland had; for at least fifteen years the standard was to take it from the hip. He also said that Holland's treatment would have been dangerous if Jon had stayed on those three drugs for longer than six months.

He wondered if Holland interpreted the pathology tests himself, instead of having them read by a board-certified pathologist. That's exactly what had happened. Holland told Jon he had multiple myeloma half an hour after taking bone marrow from his sternum. A bone core biopsy would have taken two days to interpret, but Holland wasn't willing to wait. Jon walked out of that appointment with an immediate diagnosis.

We sought out a myeloma expert in Minneapolis, who said he didn't think Jon had been misdiagnosed because Dr. Holland was well respected and regarded as an expert. But he respected Jon's Minnesota doctors too. The average survival is 2½ to 3 years, this doctor said. He and his fellow oncologists can help patients make it to three to five years, but ten-year survival "comes out of the blue," he said. "There's very little evidence that it has anything to do with anything we've done."

Jon asked if the doctor still tells people this cancer is incurable. "I don't think it's incurable," he replied, "but I don't know how to cure it."

Jon wrote to Dr. Holland. He wrote back immediately, expressing pleasure that Jon was doing so well. He said several other patients who received the same mix of Melphalan, Prednisone, and Interferon were also doing well. "I can assure you that your slides were looked at in a careful and proper fashion," he wrote. He concluded, "I wish you a long life."

Next Jon asked his current Minnesota doctor why he should be suspicious of the original diagnosis. "I don't know why you should be skeptical," he wrote in the margin of the letter. "However I am, even though Dr. Holland was obviously an authority."

Then new evidence emerged. Jon's medical file from Maine showed that the pathology report on the bone core biopsy that Holland would not wait two days for had actually concluded, "No evidence of myeloma." In a letter to Jon's Maine family doctor Holland said that he was discontinuing treatment after six months because Jon had shown no improvement. But now, in his letter to Jon, he was saying Jon's myeloma "had improved after treatment." Both statements could not be true.

Oh, yes, I was angry. I was angry that this doctor recklessly put us through twelve years of living life on the edge. What doctor gives you "six to twelve years" to live anyway? What doctor diagnoses you on a Thursday and begins chemotherapy on Monday—rushing headlong into treatment. But when you are the patient you don't know any better. You want to get rid of this thing that's going to kill you. What doctor continues chemotherapy, which is dangerous when you don't actually have cancer, for six months after he gets a biopsy report that states that you do not have cancer?

People who heard Jon's story sometimes asked if he intended to sue. He always said "absolutely not." He considered himself lucky to be alive. In a study of 1,500 patients with this cancer, only forty-four were alive after ten years. "How many of those people would have loved to trade places with me?" he asked. He quoted Bruce Springsteen: "It ain't no sin to be glad you're alive." When Jon's tennis partner, a lawyer, asked him if he'd thought about suing, Jon said he hadn't but was curious, "Would I have a good case?" "Donna would have a better one," our friend replied.

In his darkest moments, he believed having the cancer cloud over his head was appropriate punishment for neglecting Darcy. It was a menacing cloud. I was on constant watch, worried that any minor health problem might mean a flare-up of the cancer. I developed a fatalistic view of life. Whenever I thought of something I might do in the future, I told myself, "Nah, I'll be dead by then," equating Jon's death with my own. I balked at saving for retirement. "Why bother? We might not get to retirement." By focusing so intensely on Jon I neglected Darcy too, and I also feel guilty about that.

I remember Dr. Holland now as a rip-roaring narcissist in pink Tom Wolfe-ian suits, so consumed by his reputation, so wrapped up in himself, that he felt he could bypass standard medical practices and do whatever he damn well pleased. After all, it's easy to "cure" patients when they don't have cancer.

Twelve years—the end of our six-to-twelve-year death sentence—passed with little notice by either of us. One by one, all four of our parents had died over a two-year period. The mystery cancer had given way to the reality of death.

Chapter 25

Portland awakened my professional skills. It also exposed me to the joy of sports for the first time in my life. Peterson—and most other towns—had no sports for girls in the late 1950s and early 1960s. Years later, in my thirties, when Jon first asked me to join him in a pickup softball game, I refused. I had a few deficiencies: I couldn't throw, catch, or hit.

But I eventually showed up for games because I felt keenly my lack of opportunity as a kid. I thought, "I come from an athletic family, so the genes must be there somewhere." They were well hidden, as it turned out. Once, when I was playing second base, a newcomer to our games asked another player, "Why is that woman throwing underhand?" as I shoveled a ball to third as best I could. "Maybe she wanted to avoid hitting the runner," our third baseman said gallantly. He should have said, "Because she can't throw overhand."

But once I was willing to risk embarrassment, I was seriously interested in learning how to play this game. I paid close attention to what was going on in the field, and I got better. But I still didn't have the instincts of guys who'd played out of the cradle. Once, when I was pitching, I was backing up the catcher while a runner came in. I caught the ball and tagged the runner. My brain went into joy mode, "Great! I've gotten an out. Good for me!" But the runner had upended our catcher, and in typical motherly fashion, I went to pick her up and dust her off—while another run scored.

Here is part of what I wrote in a Portland newspaper column:

> It's nearly beyond [male athletes'] comprehension that for some of us, even no-fault office softball t'aint that easy. By "us," I mean the generation of women for whom all team

sports have been spectator sports, and who have missed the camaraderie, the bonding that goes with participation in organized athletics. Even if we've played tennis or golf, we longtime watchers don't have the instincts, we don't have the moves for team sports.

So when we stride onto the softball field at a relatively advanced age, we first pray the ball won't come to us. We make arrangements with the nearest big guy with obvious competence to "cover" for us. At some point we advance to where we'd at least try to make the catch, to gamble for the thrill of victory or the agony of defeat.

But the willingness doesn't erase the terror as the ball plummets out of the sky toward us. All we can think about is getting the ball into our super-scooper glove and keeping it there. We forget what our male teammates know instinctively: that the game goes on after the catch, that somewhere a runner may be advancing while we smile at the ball resting snugly amid the leather.

It turned out that it didn't matter how well I played. The big deal was being there. We played at a beautiful oceanfront park near our Cape Elizabeth house, but later, as we became established in our collective eccentricities, we played other teams at other fields. Jon was "the commissioner" who called everybody Sunday mornings and convinced them to shirk their family obligations to come out and play. We were a hodgepodge of players from the news media and a bunch of devoted hangers-on, including a big guy we called Kong.

In a game with Governor Joe Brennan's team, with Brennan pitching, Kong slammed a line drive into the Governor's chest. He grunted and lurched sideways. A collective gasp spread across the field. We thought we'd killed him. But he caught his breath and recovered. Kong apologized. I'm sure the Governor was surprised when Kong told him he wasn't in the media but made pizza at a bar we sometimes went to after games.

In one of our pickup games I was running toward first when I collided with a fellow reporter, Pete Daly, the first baseman who was barreling toward first to get me out; his shoulder hit my jaw, upending both of us and knocking the wind out of us.

Pete wrote about it later:

Donna was at bat. Her eyes were narrowed, glinty like when the Viking is filing her battle-ax. With the first pitch she cleverly poked the ball up in the air, over the right infield. I burned rubber to get under it. Then I realized my mistake and had to change course back toward the baseline. I was approaching her at an angle. She was moving fast, like a Minnesota gopher in front of a buffalo stampede. Suddenly, too late, I realized that we were on a collision course. As the ball landed snugly in my glove I realized SHE WAS TRYING TO KILL ME! A true Daughter of Odin, this Valkyrie was determined to go to Valhalla with a gob of bloody Celtic scalp clutched in her paw.

I noticed my crazed assailant lying on the ground a few yards away. She was making a peculiar 'unh-un' sound, not unlike something I heard a female say in a movie once … So I knew right away what was up … I knew she was faking it … She was feigning injury … swelling up her jaw so's to appear in pain, trying to frame me. Here I am, knocked flatter 'n a flounder by that Norwegian Killer, who publicly tried to smash my sternum with her thick Scandinavian cranium, and now she's hogging the sympathy vote."

Each year we had a "banquet" to celebrate the season and give out awards. One year we soaked the labels off bottles of cheap champagne in our bathtub and put on our own labels. Two of our awards: "The Haley's Comet Award: Donna hit a two-run home run down the right field line with—get this—Speedy Wheels Gratz on first base to lead us to a 10-3 victory over Goodwill. This event will happen again in 76 years." That same year Jon won the "Back, Back Award: The commissioner has been telling us for years to go back, back. This year he turned forty and wishes he could go back himself."

I played several years on this coed pickup team, becoming a pitcher. It was the place I could do the least harm, given that we didn't call balls and strikes, but not necessarily the place where the least harm could be done to me. Once Jon and Phil Hoose, a regular at our games, had a contest to see who could throw a softball from the outfield closest to me without hitting me (or so they would say later) as I took my warm-up pitches. Bull's-eye! One of them landed a fly ball on my head, and I slumped to the ground. Neither took credit for the perfect throw.

Another time, when I was pitching against another team, I took a line drive to my stomach. I limped off the field, then limped back to the mound. I developed the biggest, blackest, bluest bruise in the history of softball, but none of my teammates (except Joanne Lannin) wanted to see it.

Then I joined a women team headed by Joanne, a younger colleague, generous friend, and great shortstop. She and her husband Rik O'Neal, who also worked for the paper, were stalwarts on our coed team. We joined a league, and Rik and Jon coached us. As a reporter, I was always a deadline pusher, but on game days my stories somehow got written at lightning speed.

I was both excited and nervous as game time approached. This league had good teams and good players, and I still had egregious deficiencies. A member of another team once told Joanne, "Your right fielder looks like she doesn't know what she doing, but she always catches the ball." I still couldn't throw worth a darn, so if the ball came to me, Joanne would backpedal from shortstop, I'd flip the ball to her, and she'd barrel it into the infield. I got a fair number of hits until other teams figured out that, because of my late swing, I always hit down the right field line. Win or lose, we had beer and pizza afterward. We talked, we laughed, for example about Joanne's wandering dog killing a farmer's turkey during one of our games—we reveled in our togetherness. I found out what camaraderie was.

One day Jon and I were scheduled to fly to England along with teammate Lou Ann Clifford and her husband Al Diamon, but we had a playoff game that day and we insisted on playing. Jon kept trying to get me off the field, and I kept resisting. Finally, I gave in. We called a teammate when we got to Newark Airport to find out that we had won, and that I had driven in the two winning runs. This was my greatest athletic achievement, at age forty-one! In defiance of my Peterson beginnings, I had "achieved" in sports. I also broke a Norwegian rule by bragging about it. Just a little.

I loved playing softball, but it wasn't basketball, and I never quite got over not being able to play that sport. Even at five foot two, I thought I had potential, at least in my small town. After leaving Maine, in my forties, I attended my first women's game at the

University of Minnesota. Tears streamed down my face before the game even began; they came unbidden, from someplace deep down, and there was nothing I could do to stop them. It was the first time I realized how much I had lost by not having game.

43. Softball in the snow. In defiance of my Peterson beginnings, I "achieved" in sports by playing ball. I also broke a Norwegian rule by bragging about it. Just a little.

44. Joanne Lannin, far right, and husband Rik O'Neal, next to Jon, were stalwarts on our coed team. We joined a league, and Rik and Jon coached us. As a reporter, I was always a deadline pusher, but on game days my stories somehow got written at lightning speed.

45. Joanne Lannin, my colleague. Win or lose, we had beer and pizza afterwards. We talked, we laughed, for example about Joanne's wandering dog killing a farmer's turkey during one of our games—we reveled in our togetherness. I found out what camaraderie was.

46. Fellow reporter Allen Short. Though I was a newbie at the *Strib*, Allen chose me to work with him on the 'Free to Rape' series. I was grateful to him. This would prove to be one of the most significant stories I would work on at the *Strib*. Minnesota had made an effort to deal with sex crimes. Our seven-month investigation revealed how inadequate that effort had been.

Chapter 26

hen we returned to Minneapolis from London, our dear friends, Anne and George Hage, generously asked us to house sit while they spent the summer at their lake house. It was a hot, sticky summer, and their spacious house was a cool haven on a hill with a gazebo for reading the morning paper. Barney, our beagle, whom we had left with a friend, happily joined us.

We had dinner with three *Star Tribune* reporters who said there might be one, possibly two, court reporting jobs opening up at the paper. But when I called to inquire, Managing Editor Larry Werner said there were no jobs, and if there were, they could hire someone like the guy from the Los Angeles *Times* they had just hired. Coming from a paper in Portland, Maine, I was too small potatoes for them.

This was 1989, a quarter century after my gender first made me invisible to my profession, and I still wasn't good enough. It was a difficult time. Jon was sinking into depression. The lack of a job grated on him. He felt guilty that we had left our daughter behind, along with our friends and our beloved adopted state of Maine, and for what?

I was in my midforties, and I did what any self-respecting jobless woman would do: I kicked at the door until my toes were numb and the door opened. Then I walked through. I decided to put my rage (with Norwegian Minnesota reserve, of course) into a letter to the *Star Tribune*. Jon said it was a waste of time. But I had nothing but time, so I spent the Fourth of July weekend pecking away on George's manual typewriter. I said people sometimes choose to live in smaller places for the quality of life, and that good work can be done in small places. I enclosed comments from a dozen people about my reporting for the Portland papers. Among them:

"The quality of your legal reporting is every bit as high as that which I admire in the New York *Times* and other major newspapers," said Herbert Maletz, senior judge on the U.S. Court of International Trade.

"Donna Halvorsen's story was excellent ... I am sure your paper benefits from her considerable skill," said Fred Friendly, former president of CBS News.

"Ms. Halvorsen is by far the finest court reporter I have ever encountered," said Boston trial attorney James W. Lawson.

"Sexual abuse of children has been covered over the past few years by many journalists. However, Donna Halvorsen and her contributions stand alone," said Ron Allanach, police chief of Westbrook, Maine.

A few weeks later I was heading out of state to check out jobs when Larry Werner, the editor from the *Star Tribune*, called and said, "Don't do anything before you talk to us." I'd suddenly become a hot prospect. Did my letter get their attention?

When I returned from my trip I had seven interviews over two days, then waited as summer slipped away. When the call came I was overjoyed—I had a job! And Jon soon became Managing Editor of the Macalester College alumni magazine, a job he would love.

Then I realized that the biggest paper, the paper of record, in my home state had hired me as their legal affairs reporter over six internal candidates. A little scary for Ms. Small Potatoes—this was a newsroom with 350 people—but I was ready for it. The *Star Tribune*—what we called the *Strib*— was a first-rate newspaper that shared my journalistic values. Minnesota was my progressive, squeaky-clean home state, and the paper seemed to reflect that.

But I arrived in tough times. Tensions were high. Contract negotiations were going on and there was the real possibility of a strike. As a new employee I was on probation, but City Editor Kent Gardner assured me my job was safe. I sat just in front of the hotshot from the L.A. *Times*, who went back to California after a year. I stayed seventeen.

One gracious reporter, who became a journalistic icon, welcomed me, acknowledging that he was one of the six who was passed over for my job. He would later ask me to run for union office, but I declined; I said my husband had cancer and I couldn't take on anything extra.

Another reporter, whom I knew at the journalism school, wouldn't speak to me. After three months he said he ignored me because management always thought outsiders were better qualified for good jobs than reporters already on the staff.

Jim Kelly, my first editor, calmed those early, anxious days by saying, "Have I told you lately how wonderful you are?" And, "You're one of the few people around here who doesn't drive me nuts."

My first assigned story was manna from heaven. It seemed like a perfunctory story, on one of those government reports that produce yawns, but this one would set me off on a course of reporting about domestic violence, an issue that hadn't ripened when I was covering the courts in Maine.

I was asked to write about the Minnesota Supreme Court's report on gender bias in the courts. It was an untold story, and the *Strib* gave me plenty of room to tell it. This was my lead:

> Less than a month before Joni Colsrud was to shed the bonds of an acrimonious marriage, she stepped out of her Hinckley, Minnesota trailer home into the path of her estranged husband's rage. A shotgun blast ripped through her leg. Pellets from a second shot tore a hole in her six-year-old son's shoulder.

Domestic violence emerged as the single most important issue in the report, whose lead author was Rosalie Wahl, the pioneering single mother who became the Minnesota Supreme Court's first female justice. This story had significant shock value in a state that prided itself on doing the right thing.

Colsrud was among 56,000 Minnesota women who were battered by their spouses each year, the report said. Her husband, a farmer, was free on bail for a year while she worried that he would come back and finish the job. His case came to trial only after she discovered on her own that she could file a request for a speedy trial.

If I had wanted a woman's story—and I didn't seek this one out—domestic violence was it. It was happening in cities and towns and rural farmhouses across the country, but it took place in the so-called sanctuary of the home, and it wasn't society's place to meddle. It was still a man's world in 1989, and a woman's place was in the home, no matter what happened to her there.

Orders for Protection (OFP) seemed to be the Minnesota courts' only tool, but women had difficulty getting them, they were difficult to enforce, and abusers knew how to get around them. The report cited a judge who denied a woman's request by saying that she was "the type who requested an order one day and asked to have it rescinded the next."

"I guess I need a knife in my back or at least be bleeding profusely from the head and shoulders to get an OFP," the woman was quoted as saying. "That's just about it," the judge reportedly replied.

I covered domestic violence over the years at the *Star Tribune* as understanding of it expanded and new angles emerged. It didn't just happen on the margins of society, perpetrated by drunks and losers who weren't like the rest of us. Batterers could be accountants, doctors, the guy next door—men who were verbally abusive and controlling as well as violent. This behavior had disastrous effects on women and their children, yet it was all hush-hush, or no big deal. Judges were quoted in the report as saying, "If you'd have supper on the table, this wouldn't happen," and "You've been married for ten years, you must like being hit." The message was: women just needed to learn how to behave.

Victims also were not of any particular class, or level of education, or intelligence. Jessie May was a vivacious twenty-six-year-old makeup designer who didn't see herself as someone who could be nearly killed by someone she once loved. Furious at seeing her with another man, her ex-boyfriend broke into her mother's house, threw her down a steel circular staircase until her head became like a mushy basketball, stabbed her multiple times, broke two ribs, and punctured a lung. Miraculously, she survived. A large dramatic photo in which she showed her wounds ran alongside my story. Her message was, "Love doesn't look like this."

Domestic violence was an issue I found hidden under Minnesota's good intentions. It was appalling to me, even though I certainly was aware of the second-class treatment of women and children in other situations. But after only seven weeks on the job, digging into this explosive material, my momentum stopped. I got ill with meningitis, mononucleosis, and hepatitis, origins unknown. A pain that made my head too painful to touch subsided with medication, and I went home from the hospital after four days.

I returned to the hospital ten days later with a ruptured spleen, probably caused by mono, that nearly killed me. I was out of work for six weeks, a long time for a company to support a new employee, but the *Strib* was grand, never doubted me, even sent me flowers. My physical weakness had laid me low, but I was eager to return to work, to prove that I belonged there.

§

That fall I was assigned to cover the trial of the Reverend Thomas Adamson, my first exposure to the issue of pedophile priests, and only the third such case to go to trial in the country. Like other abusive priests, Adamson had been moved from parish to parish, collecting more than two dozen victims along the way. The jury awarded a former altar boy an astounding $3.5 million, including $2.7 million in punitive damages, the largest jury award in the country, and the first assessment of punitive damages against any Catholic church body in such a case.

Two Minnesota dioceses admitted partial responsibility for the severe psychological damage Adamson inflicted on the altar boy beginning when he was thirteen. Still, church attorneys were shocked by the size of the punitive damages, which were subsequently reduced to $137,000. But the very possibility of punitive damages put the church hierarchy around the country on high alert.

St. Paul attorney Jeff Anderson, who brought the church to its knees in this case, went on to become the most prominent advocate for survivors of priest abuse in the country. Though I did not continue to cover this story after the trial, child sexual abuse in the Catholic church of course went on to become an important issue around the globe for more than a decade, and still has reverberations today.

§

Sex crimes once again landed on my plate in a big way when reporter Allen Short asked me to work with him on a project that came to be called "Free to Rape." It was another introduction to the dark underside of Minnesota criminal law. Whenever I had looked at a neglected issue while covering the courts in Maine, it always seemed to me that Minnesota was the state that had done something about it. When I got to Minnesota, and began to look at such issues close up, I discovered that the Legislature sometimes passed a law and considered the job done, without solving the problem at all.

Minnesota, like all the other states, had done practically nothing about domestic violence. But with sex crimes it had made a valiant effort. Our investigation revealed how unsuccessful that effort had been. We were shocked to find how lenient Minnesota was on rapists and child molesters. Twenty-seven percent of the worst offenders didn't go to prison at all, our reporting showed. Those who did, served an average of two years. The average rapist had been charged with more than three sex crimes; the average child molester with more than four; but those were just the times they were caught. We knew that in most cases they had committed more. One offender I interviewed said he had molested fifty-two boys.

Minnesota was unusual in that it sent many offenders to "treatment" instead of prison, a seemingly humane approach that won praise for the state. Having made a name for itself as a pioneer in alcohol and drug treatment—the famed Hazelden Foundation's original venue in Center City, Minnesota, created the model for such treatment—Minnesota became treatment heaven. It occasionally even sent check bouncers to "treatment," and it wanted to be a pioneer in rehabilitating sex offenders, an admirable goal. But this was a tough business. The behavior of most perpetrators was deeply ingrained, and the state wasn't making much headway in changing it. Still, the Legislature continued to pump large amounts of money into the effort at rehabilitation without ever studying whether all that money was accomplishing anything.

We didn't anticipate the major finding of our seven-month study: offenders who had undergone treatment were more likely to reoffend than those who had not! (We found this out through computer-assisted reporting, the first such project undertaken on any topic by any newspaper.) The treatment advocates at the University of Minnesota were unhappy with us. They needed continued funding so they could keep treating offenders and figure out how to do it successfully. No one outside the program seemed to know that treatment seldom worked. At a conference I asked John Money, a nationally respected pro-treatment professional, what percentage of offenders could be successfully treated. "Fifteen percent," he replied. While progressive Minnesota didn't do everything right, the unfortunate truth was that no one else had figured out what to do with sex offenders either.

Our work, spread over fifteen pages, caused quite a stir. Minnesotans told us in a poll that they wanted judges to impose much longer sentences on sex offenders, and many would pay higher taxes to do so. The Legislature had lengthened sentences just two years earlier, but to a public sickened by recent high-profile crimes it wasn't enough.

The Legislature scrambled to make amends, and I covered its efforts, including passage of a "psychopathic personality" law (later called the "sexually dangerous person" law), that allowed the most incorrigible offenders to be locked up indefinitely *after* serving their sentences. The law was challenged in the courts but the Minnesota Supreme Court found it to be constitutional after a remand from the U.S. Supreme Court.

The story was my first exposure to big-time investigative journalism and major market awards, neither of which I aspired to when I was on the outside looking in. We won first place for investigative reporting from Minnesota's Society of Professional Journalists, the Newswriting Sweepstakes Award from the Minnesota Associated Press Association, a Certificate of Merit in the American Bar Association's National Media Awards Program, and a "laurel" from the Columbia Journalism Review. *Star Tribune* editor Tim McGuire called it "one of the most important and distinguished projects we've ever undertaken." My months of working with reporter Allen Short, our editor Ron Meador, and intern/computer whiz Dan Eggen, was a good experience, something I'd remember fondly later on, when project reporting became a horror.

§

My next assignment took me off the legal affairs beat and sent me to the Capitol to cover the Legislature's effort to pass a major health care law. In 1992 Minnesota already had more health programs for its residents than most states, but thousands were shut out by high costs and inequities imposed by insurance companies. Minnesota's reform effort was carried out by a bipartisan group of legislators known as the Gang of Seven—bipartisanship being the only way anything could get done because of the enormous power of the health insurance lobby. It was truly a pioneering effort, and the whole world was watching. After the law was passed, I briefed a Chinese delegation on it.

What I discovered was that in the early 1990s health insurance did not exist to cover people. It existed to *not* cover them. From the industry's point of view, health insurance was for healthy people. That's how they made money. If you had health problems— presumably the reason you would need insurance in the first place—nobody wanted to insure you. This was the "pre-existing condition" problem that would loom large in health care debates over the next twenty-five years and was one of the main targets of the Affordable Care Act. I also discovered that women paid more for health insurance than men because they have the babies.

Soaring costs had priced many people out of the market, so cost containment became a major goal. Republican Governor Arne Carlson vetoed the first bill as too costly, but he vowed to work with the Gang of Seven on a new version. That was good news. It meant the next bill wouldn't necessarily be vetoed.

The Minnesota Hospital Association and the Minnesota Medical Association opposed the bill, in part because it included a provider fee, and in part because of the lurking potential for a single payer system. Thousands of nurses supported the bill.

The original idea was to provide universal health care. That plan was scaled back because of cost. When the bill was short of votes to pass the House, Carlson's lobbying of Republicans put the effort over the top. Two Democrats, Senator Linda Berglin and Representative Paul Ogren, were titans in this effort. But the other five legislators in the Gang of Seven were also highly committed, and the chemistry of the group helped produce a bill. The Gang met in secret, which rankled opponents but shielded the group from lobbyists. "We did take them by surprise," a member said afterward. "It's a real dangerous way to do business," said one close observer, "but it was the only way this thing was going to happen." None of them could have imagined that it would take courage to pass a health care bill, but Republican Senator Duane Benson found that out: his family received death threats.

In the end, HealthRight, renamed MinnesotaCare, passed. The bill didn't provide universal health care, but it was ambitious, with goals of containing costs and improving quality while providing basic affordable care for all.

When the Clinton administration began its push for universal healthcare, it brought in Minnesota experts as advisers. But the health insurance lobby, with power that in my experience was exceeded only by the tobacco lobby, shut down the effort in no time flat. The industry may have been caught off guard in Minnesota, but when the Clintons put the issue on the national stage, it was ready. And nobody, but nobody—perhaps especially Hillary Clinton—could have accomplished anything under that pressure. The public wasn't ready to be led by a strong woman who stepped out of the demure role of First Lady and didn't bake cookies.

§

For a time I went back to the legal affairs beat, which I loved, but after six years it was becoming too hard to hear in courtrooms. Though I had fairly sophisticated hearing aids, I needed to turn them up as high as possible in order to hear in court, and that made me nauseous. It was also exhausting to strain to hear for hours at a time. When a new job covering consumer issues was created, I jumped at it.

About this time, women in the newsroom discovered that the *Strib* had been paying men and women unequally. It was a union newspaper that supposedly paid its employees according to Newspaper Guild scales, but our union leader, Marg Zack, a reporter and a lawyer, discovered that because the newspaper gave some men "merit" raises on top of the scales, many men made way more than we women did—$500 a week over scale for a few of them.

Management, caught in an embarrassing discriminatory practice, moved quickly to make amends, giving raises to me and other women. Additional raises were forthcoming as the legal case we initiated moved sluggishly forward.

One day I was sitting in a pod with three male colleagues when one of them asked if I'd gotten a raise. I said I had. One of the guys jumped up from his chair and said, "You're not better than me!" and stormed off. I knew he'd had problems of his own, but he had never been a woman twenty-four seven, never spent a lifetime being subjected to views on his worthiness by the opposite sex, never been denied access to the profession because of gender. He apologized without my having to explain any of that—such explanations didn't register with male newspaper types anyway—and we returned to peaceful pod life, no lessons learned.

47. St. Paul attorney Jeff Anderson, who brought the church to its knees in this case, went on to become the most prominent advocate for survivors of priest abuse in the country. Though I did not continue to cover this story after the trial, child sexual abuse in the Catholic Church of course went on to become an important issue around the globe for more than a decade, and still has reverberations today.

Chapter 27

ucian Filip, intense and charming, was the first. Nine other journalists from around the globe followed. It was all Jon's doing. He worked at Macalester College in St. Paul, where the World Press Institute (WPI) was based. WPI ran a Fellowship program that brought journalists from all over the world to immerse themselves in American culture and explore issues of global journalism. Jon suggested we apply to be a host family. We did, and our lives were upended in a magnificent way.

Lucian, a Romanian in his early thirties, got his views of the U.S. from watching *Dallas*. Despite that, he became known as the philosopher of that first group. He wondered if every American had a "mowing machine." He wondered, as we drove through Minneapolis' neighborhoods, why there were houses but no people outside them.

He asked, "What do Americans want? Is it money? Is it education?" as if we were all the same.

He asked, "What does it mean when a woman walks up to you and says, 'Hi'?" Coming from a Communist country, he distrusted even such a benign overture.

The WPI Fellows program brought eight to ten journalists to the U.S. each year for a four-month, expenses-paid tour of the country. They went to small Minnesota towns, where editors and their families showed them small town life and the workings of community newspapers. They stayed with rural families, who showed them farm life.

Over a decade we became host parents to ten journalists from eight countries: Nigeria, South Africa, India, Bangladesh, Ireland, Argentina, Panama, and Romania. Our job as hosts was to introduce them to the Twin Cities and help them with their needs and questions.

It was fun to learn about the fellows' cultures and their lives as journalists and, especially, to watch them interact joyfully with each other. My favorite cultural story is about Hafiz Imam of Bangladesh, who emailed his mother shortly after he arrived, "Have had my first American meal, hot dog." His mother emailed back, "I don't care if it's hot or cold, don't eat dog." She found him a wife while he was gone.

Another of our fellows was Oliver Kiss, an ethnic Hungarian from Romania. Oliver was a reporter/photographer/part owner of a newspaper that existed to keep the Hungarian culture and ethnicity alive. He was twenty-seven, bright, witty, and poor. He made eighty-four dollars a month, lived with his parents, and had an uncanny ability to make friends.

When he and Jon were on a bike ride one Saturday, they came across guys playing frisbee in a park. Oliver had never seen a frisbee, never heard of the game, but soon was playing. When we invited him for beer and pizza the next night he said, "I'll tell the others." We didn't mean to invite eight other frisbee players, but we were delighted when some came.

Nothing prepared us for Cordelia Onu, our fifth journalist. Cordelia was thirty-three years old, an editor on a newspaper in Lagos, Nigeria. Our first dinner together, right after she arrived, was painful for all three of us. We thought we were being our low-key Norwegian selves, but we thought that we had overwhelmed her. We realized later that she was simply exhausted from her long trip. When she recalled that dinner she wrote, "I was asleep with my two eyes open at the first meeting. It was midnight in Lagos and my body fully reflected that, I barely heard anything they said, but I felt their love and kindness."

She quickly bonded with the other African in the group, Japhet Sanga from Tanzania, who had a courtly presence and a wonderful sense of humor. He gets credit for the relationship we ended up having with Cordelia. When we invited her to a picnic on a hill overlooking a Minneapolis lake, she asked if Japhet could come along. He made her laugh, brought her out of herself, and filled every lull in the conversation.

Afterward, he said he told Cordelia that she had "the best host parents in the program" and should treat us as if we were her own parents. After that, she left a message on Jon's Macalester voice mail saying, "I know that somehow I've been a bit detached from you and Donna. It's not because I have anything against you or anybody. The thing is, I've become so used to being on my own and being with just my family ... But if it's hurting at all, or maybe you think that something is wrong, I want to say that nothing is really wrong ... So just tell Donna that everything is okay."

Cordelia could have been president of her country if it weren't such a war-torn mess, or, I'm convinced, head of the United Nations. Kofi Annan, a Macalester student from Ghana, became U.N. Secretary General. Jon and I went to Norway when he received the Nobel Peace Prize.

Cordelia was married, with three children. She was funny and articulate beyond words. When we talked to her on the phone we always said, "Give our best to Japhet." At one point Cordelia asked him, "Japhet, what have you done to these people?" She knew he was becoming one of our "children" as well. Japhet was engaged. He negotiated the "bride price"—the number of cows he would have to give the parents of his fiancé—by email on Jon's work computer.

After taking classes and acclimating themselves in St. Paul, the fellows set off on a cross-country tour that would show them more of the U.S. than most Americans ever see, from the White House to the California redwoods and lots in between.

In August Cordelia emailed us: "I am sure you must be wondering what kind of daughter I am. Sorry for the long silence from my end. I called from Custer Park (in Montana) but I wasn't sure anyone got the message. I spoke to a machine. I am fine and enjoying the trip ... My family in Nigeria is saying a big thank you to the kind family looking after their mummy here."

I emailed back: "It was wonderful to hear from you. You must wonder what kind of mummy I am, letting her daughter wander around this strange country without a note of encouragement now and then. My regards to Japhet."

Cordelia emailed after the group had been to Nashville and Memphis: "I didn't go to Graceland. I would have loved to, only that I was scared I might get hooked to the 'King' like millions of people around the world. He has enough following as it is. I saw part of his life story at the Country Music Hall of Fame and I have listened to his music, but I don't understand him at all."

She emailed Jon on his birthday: "Happy birthday!!! And like we say in Igboland, 'May you live to see your great- grandchildren, and may you live to see your fondest dreams come true.'"

When the fellows returned to St. Paul in October, they had a busy two weeks before returning to their home countries. On the last weekend Japhet, Cordelia, and Radhika Dhawan (from India) came to dinner. Luckily, we seated Radhika between Cordelia and Japhet, because her peace-keeping efforts were needed. The subject was homosexuality and the AIDS epidemic. Japhet said that AIDS was spread only by heterosexual sex and that homosexuality did not exist in Tanzania, which enraged Cordelia.

The longer he stood his ground, the more she assailed him. Radhika tried to intervene when Cordelia roared, "He's a typical African male—he doesn't know anything!" Japhet, sweet-tempered fellow that he is, let her criticism wash over him. Finally, Jon walked behind Japhet, put his hands on his shoulders and said, "Japhet, my man, there is a saying in America, that you have to 'know when to hold 'em and when to fold 'em,' and I think the time has come for you to fold 'em."

Several days later, referring to our evening together, Japhet said, "Cordelia was ignorant ..." I interrupted and said, "Oh, no, here we go again." But we were at a rather proper farewell lunch, and Cordelia remained demure, saying nothing. They parted wonderful friends. At the farewell dinner my poor hearing prevented me from catching what Cordelia said from the podium, but Jon wrote it down for me:

> My host mother, Donna Halvorsen, did something I will never forget. I left her a message telling her that I was freezing [in the hotel where the group was staying] and asked her if she could bring some warm clothes on Thursday [in two days, when I was going to meet her at the *Star Tribune*.] I had no sooner hung up the phone when she arrived at the Day's Inn with all kinds of warm clothes. No one has ever responded to my needs so immediately except my mother, my biological mother.

Who knows what effect simple gestures can have? Sometimes it doesn't even take a gesture. Rohit Saran, our Indian fellow, whose parents were in an arranged marriage, told us we had shown him "how a husband and wife can be friends."

Cordelia said at the ceremony that before she left home a Nigerian who had been in the program gave her the names of "his people" in St. Paul. She looked at the names, Lee Kaplan and Judy Strom, and replied at the time, "These are not your people—they're not even Nigerian." But she said she realized as she went through the program that, "Now I have people here."

After 9/11 Cordelia wrote to us:

> How has it been all this while? This is to let you know that you are not alone in your nation's trying moment. We here feel for you and as a nation also have our own mourning to do. So far we have counted ninety-four Nigerians missing, and for some reasons we fear that the real figure will be thrice that number. A Nigerian-owned security outfit provides personnel for so many of the companies at the World Trade Center, and so we fear a very high casualty figure. I hope you are all fine and taking this in your stride. I admire your spirit as a nation and the way everyone is involved in helping out. That's how things should be. I can't even begin to imagine how shocked you people are. This is new to you, and it is a rude way of welcoming you to the horrors we are constantly faced with in the rest of the world. Here we are so used to calamity that we end up sounding hard and appearing unfeeling. We often do all we can to acquire a very thick skin or else we spend every moment crying.
>
> I have seen more than enough sorrows and been through horrible situations. I was born close to the civil war in my country and the very first things I can recall are the desperate dashes into the forest late at night and fearful air raids. The war ended close to my fourth birthday, and I can clearly remember the ragged, vermin-ridden malnourished little fatherless girl that I was, lining up with a dirty tin to collect food being given out by UNICEF. Somehow we often find the courage and will power to put all these behind us and live, though some of the images from early days still

haunt me now. You will survive this, both as individuals and as a nation, and you will be the better for that.

The program's end each year was heartrending because of the strong bonds we had developed. At the airport Rohit reached down and touched Jon's feet, the Indian gesture of respect for one's elders.

Oliver was just Oliver right to the end. There was little going on when we took him to the airport so he had the time to spend charming two ticket agents. Without the charm, the skinny Hungarian wearing a Stetson hat he'd bought in Texas might have been viewed with suspicion. Not Oliver. After he had checked in, we waited for Finnish journalist Kaius Niemi, who was leaving on the same plane. As Kaius handed over his ticket, the agent pointed at Oliver and said, "Do you know *him*?" Kaius reached down on his luggage cart, retrieved a Stetson hat and put it on his head. That was his answer.

Many years later, after Jon died, Cordelia wrote to me:

The WPI host parents are a group of very hospitable, dynamic, long-suffering Americans who get to meet and parent an old child from a strange new country every year. They seem to enjoy it, which baffles me. They allow total strangers they just met to roam their houses. They spend good dollars on these 'children' and follow them up with endless calls as they go off on the road trip portion of the program. Isn't that how parenting goes?

You get to learn more things about the country from the parents than you would ever learn in a classroom. They represent the Real America. They stick to you for life. I still have not gotten over their love and large-heartedness. I still recall the couple who returned me to childhood at the ripe old age of thirty-three.

48. Japhet Sanga from Tanzania had a courtly presence and a wonderful sense of humor. He gets credit for the relationship we ended up having with Cordelia. When we invited her to a picnic on a hill overlooking a Minneapolis lake, she asked if Japhet could come along. He made her laugh, brought her out of herself, and filled every lull in the conversation.

49. Cordelia Onu, the fifth WPI Fellow Jon and I hosted, was thirty-three years old, an editor on a newspaper in Lagos, Nigeria. She could have been president of her country if it weren't such a war-torn mess, or, I'm convinced, head of the United Nations, like Kofi Annan, a Macalester student from Ghana. Cordelia, married, with three children, was funny and articulate beyond words.

50. Jim Buchta (above) and Karen Youso were experts on houses. As the consumer reporter, I joined them in an investigation that had shocking results: Half of new Minnesota homes had serious moisture problems, shoddy construction practices and other defects that could cost half their value to repair.

Chapter 28

Investigative reporting was off my radar when I started out. Nothing about it appealed to me. I wanted to write *nice* stories about people, not dig up dirt on them and confront them with it. We girls who grew up in small Norwegian towns in the 1950s were raised to be inoffensive, if not invisible.

But the "Free to Rape" project opened me up to it. It was a good job for a reporter who liked poking into dusty records and doing research on the internet, and it was easier for a person with defective ears. The *Star Tribune* was a good newspaper. It did a good job of reporting the daily news in a metropolitan area of 3.5 million people, and of looking below the surface to find wrongdoing. This was elementary: It is the newspaper's job to point out when society's norms are being violated at the expense of the public interest.

Especially when it involves something as basic as the roofs over our heads. It was a shock to discover that Minnesota's home construction industry was knowingly building substandard houses, leaving thousands of people with wrecked homes, depleted life savings, and emotional devastation.

I knew from my Capitol reporting that legislators resisted passing anything supposedly harmful to business, and that included builders. Legislators took what lobbyists told them as gospel. The few homeowners who complained were told it took a year or so for building materials to dry out, which was true, and that any remaining problems were caused by their failure to maintain their homes, which was not true. No one saw fit to tell home buyers that their new houses could decompose around them and make them

147

sick in a few short years. There was no lobby for homeowners and no accountability for home builders.

Our focus started with a smaller story about older houses and airport noise. My colleague, Karen Youso, was an indefatigable reporter who always had her nose to the ground for stories. She got this one from a neighbor on a playground near her south Minneapolis home.

Minneapolis, a city of incomparable beauty, had a terrible problem with airport noise. As the population and air traffic grew, life in neighborhoods near the airport became intolerable. The neighborhoods closest to the airport had 1950s houses, generally small but well maintained. The Metropolitan Airports Commission (MAC) bought the houses and razed hundreds of them without causing much of a stir. But when complaints came from more affluent neighborhoods, the MAC came up with a new idea. It would insulate homes against noise: stuff the walls with insulation, install new doors and windows and furnaces. Maybe people would forget they couldn't go outside to deadhead their daisies in midday without being deafened by airplanes flying overhead.

The MAC was a quasi-public entity, but it was run like a private fiefdom with little if any oversight, and saving money was important to them, even though they had lots of it. So when they decided to generously "give" homeowners these "upgrades" to their homes, they also decided to do it on the cheap. They did not ventilate the houses, even though two experts told them they would endanger the occupants' health if they sealed these homes up tight without ventilating them.

In old drafty houses, carbon monoxide—the byproduct of combustion—could escape through leaky walls and windows, but when houses were tightened up, the dangerous gas could be trapped inside and poison people. Nobody had died at the time we wrote our story, but it was a very real possibility.

The story won first place for investigative reporting from Minnesota's Society of Professional Journalists. In response to it, the MAC ventilated the houses and went back to claiming it was a national trendsetter in dealing with airport noise.

That story set us off on a course of reporting on houses that was unique in the country. After the MAC story appeared, Karen's sources kept telling her, "You think old houses have problems? You should look at new ones." Our editor, Jim Fuller, agreed. He encouraged Karen to push beyond the MAC story to this unprecedented—and very dramatic—area of inquiry. Karen talked to business reporter Jim Buchta, and they agreed that looking into the quality of newly built homes was a story the *Strib* should tell. Jim and Karen were both experts on houses and were, in fact, the only people in the newsroom who could tell this story and get it right. Jim had written hundreds of stories about houses and the building industry. As the longtime writer of the Fixit column, Karen had answered hundreds of homeowners' questions about their houses. Both were ahead of the curve in their knowledge of building practices, materials, trends, and problems. They had just never put it all together before in the case of new homes. Now they would. As the paper's consumer reporter, I joined the effort.

Karen and I validated our premise by attending an alternative building conference in Chicago attended by state officials, builders, and housing advocates looking for ways to build better houses. Karen knew these people, and they knew her, which meant everybody would talk to us. We quickly discovered that what we'd heard was true—that today's new homes were poorly built, but it was mostly a secret. Builders kept building them, and people kept buying them.

Karen and I barely knew each other at that point, so we told each other our life stories over dinner in the Parker House bar. Like girls at a slumber party, we continued talking long after we returned to our room—until an Illinois state trooper in full regalia knocked on our door to say the neighbors were complaining about "the noise." He seemed embarrassed to find two women in their jammies— Karen in her forties, me in my fifties—who said they were "just talking."

We returned home from Chicago with a national story, eager to plunge in. But management pushed back. Big projects take a long time; they always involve wrangling and sometimes shifts in direction. It is management's job to ask tough questions, and they did that in this case. This was a huge powerful industry that had not been challenged before. But somehow, their objections seemed personal. Did management not respect our expertise? Was it too big for the likes of us? Sometimes it felt as if we were being treated like naughty children, though we were in our thirties, forties, and fifties. Our conclusion: They did not trust the three of us, nor our editor, Jim Fuller. We were not the stars of the *Star Tribune* newsroom.

This was one of the biggest stories I had ever worked on, and it turned out to be the worst experience I ever had producing a story. My reputation in the newsroom, the respect and support I had enjoyed in the front office since the beginning, seemed to evaporate when the story was assigned to the newly hired projects editor— let's call him Ralph Restak.

He took Jim Fuller off editing and tried to remove Jim Buchta and me from the project and work only with Karen. He made us engage in silly exercises, whether to harass us or because he was marching to a drumbeat that we couldn't hear. All of this felt like unimaginable insults to our team of experienced professionals.

Thankfully, there were three of us. We had an unspoken agreement that this was our story, and we would see it through. Each of us lost it, ready to give up, at different times, and the other two were always there to resuscitate. As I felt myself becoming depressed, I should have left the project, but that was unthinkable. We'd done an exhaustive search, and we knew that if we ever got the story into the newspaper, we would be the first reporters in North America to tell it. Though it was an arduous, uphill struggle, in the end we did get the story into the paper, with stellar copy editing by Sharon Emery.

We found that 50 percent of new Minnesota homes had problems in the first three to five years that could cost half their value to repair: serious moisture problems, shoddy construction practices, and improperly installed water heaters and furnaces that could malfunction, possibly sickening their occupants. In fact, Karen was overcome by carbon monoxide while she was looking at a water heater with an indoor air quality expert.

It was a great urban legend that the state building code would protect home buyers, but the code didn't guarantee a high-quality, lasting house, or even one that wouldn't decompose around them. It provided a minimal standard, and it lagged behind scientific knowledge on how to build healthy, durable homes, because builders repeatedly shot down changes to the codes. The entire system was run by the building industry, nationally as well as in Minnesota, with complicity by legislatures. It might take years for defects to surface, and then anyone who might have been expected to accept responsibility said, "Not my problem." Homeowners were left with repair bills that were often in the hundreds of thousands of dollars.

Expensive houses were not immune. Karen once stood on the shoulders of a building official at an open house to collect mold from the rafters of a $1 million home. Requiring ventilation, the industry claimed, would make houses unaffordable. This was another urban legend. The builder of this house said he didn't build to a higher standard—i.e., with mechanical ventilation—because it would have cost $8,000 more—less than one percent of the sale price.

We thought, "They will get it. They just don't get it now." They didn't want to build bad houses, we decided—they were confused and arrogant. They were comfortable with their profits and locked into building practices that had worked for them before. They thought of themselves as the keepers of the American dream, but they were failing miserably.

The problems actually began with the national push for energy efficiency in the 1970s. In Minnesota and elsewhere the shells of houses were tightened up to keep cold air out, but that also trapped moist air inside walls, which interacted with new composite wood products that deteriorated when exposed to moisture.

Minnesota builder groups knew that mechanical ventilation would solve the problem but fought it fiercely for years. As a result, thousands of Minnesota houses were built to a lower standard, relying on air leaks and open windows for ventilation—even in winter—and left to rot. In some houses the problem became apparent when mushrooms grew out of walls. Having a "good" builder didn't necessarily help. Few builders did more than the building code required.

After the publication of our stories Joe Lstiburek, one of the country's best-known building scientists, told us, "I'm honored to meet the three people who will change how houses are built in this country." He said he had been trying to influence the quality of housing for twenty years, but that we three had accomplished more with our series than he did in all those years. Many of today's building standards have his fingerprints on them. We called him "the rock star of building science."

"Today has been like watching fireworks," one of our state government sources said when our first stories appeared. "You guys really know how to get people's attention."

The following year an administrative law judge approved a set of sweeping rules that would affect the design, construction, and operation of nearly all houses built in Minnesota. Builders had worked on the development of the new code but in the end they would not support it. It required mechanical ventilation in all new houses and imposed other rules that the judge said would significantly improve the durability of houses and protect the health of their occupants. It was believed to be the most stringent code in the country.

Jim Fuller told us, "You have achieved something considerably greater than most people manage to do in their entire careers. It's been hell, but the result is stupendous. It will have a major impact on the lives of hundreds of thousands, perhaps millions, of people over many years. It's a privilege to work with you."

Though the process was hellish, the *Star Tribune* gave us the platform to tell this important story. To their credit, upper management kept us going for nearly a year, putting up the considerable money that the story cost. But it would not have happened without our tough-mindedness, our colleagues' support, and our sources, who kept telling us, "You've got the story, and you've got it right. Don't give up!"

We also, we three, enjoyed our work together, finding an unusual chemistry. "It was just like a treasure hunt," Jim said. "We didn't know where the story would end up. It just unraveled in a really wonderful way." The quality that Jim and Karen had in common that so appealed to me—besides their obvious knowledge and strong reporting skills—was character, enormous character. These stories involved science and math, not my strong suits. But I had two great teachers, with great personalities, and in the end, it was a joy to work with them and master a new subject.

§

I lasted to the end of the project, but after a year of working under constant pressure on a high-profile story, a year of conflict with the editor who supervised our work, I crashed. My colleagues knew I was at the end of my tether when Restak breezed by my cubicle one afternoon, saying something obnoxious on his way—I was so fed up that I went down to the women's locker room and put my head under the shower. My primary care physician, Joel, told me that I was not going to make it to retirement in such a toxic work environment. He gave me medication to keep me going, but said I needed to get a new job. I had pushed myself through a deepening depression with help from Jim, Karen, and my therapist, Jo. She told me I expected too much of myself. She knew all four of Jon's and my parents had died in a two-year period, and she had helped me through that crisis. When I went to tell the paper's administrative editor that I needed a leave, my colleague Ingrid Sundstrom went with me, a good thing because when I opened my mouth, I couldn't speak.

I took a four-month paid leave. The rest did me a world of good, but unfortunately my problems with editor Restak resumed on day one, when I returned to the newsroom and his greeting wasn't, "Donna, how are you?" Instead, he yelled from across the newsroom, where he was jawing with reporters, "Hey, Donna, how many times did we rewrite that lead—fifty?"

We continued to cross swords in a series of incidents that made my last year at the *Strib* not a happy or healthy time for me. He didn't like my writing. He didn't like me. He said that Managing Editor Pam Fine told him to supervise me personally because I was "error prone." But Fine knew me; she knew that was not true. Having been hearing impaired since birth, I'd made very few errors throughout my career because I worked so hard at hearing: listening intently, reading lips, taking great notes, triple-checking facts, and using special devices—without help from any management, anywhere, in thirty-two years.

Once when Karen and I did make an error, Restak ordered us to Fine's office to be disciplined. Disciplined? This isn't how errors in stories are handled. The newsroom was in an uproar. We were chastised for the mistake, which actually happened because he pushed a story into print despite our warning him that it was not yet ready. He was not chastised, even though we had caught him in a lie in the meeting with Fine, and she was well aware of it. I shared Karen's view: "It was so obvious that if we were men, we wouldn't be treated like this. If they had treated a couple of male reporters this way they would have thrown their computers on the floor and walked out."

Once he wrote his own version of one of my stories, a violation of union rules, and the union wanted me to testify against him. I declined. I was sure new episodes were ahead. I didn't have the stomach to relive old ones.

Throughout my time at the *Star Tribune* I had flare-ups of the gastrointestinal illness that had begun so many years before in Albany. Eventually I had surgery to prevent the cancer that my gastroenterologist said was inevitable in a year or two. I was out of work for two months. When I returned to work Restak sent me to human resources to get me put on disability leave because I had been sick so much. The HR director listened sympathetically and did nothing.

Although an editor can make a reporter's life miserable, I knew that in the end, this editor had no power over me. No one in management would have fired me—period—and certainly not on his recommendation. I was well established in my job, had won major awards, and was admired by reporters, editors, and staff. One colleague told me I was her model for beat reporting. Another colleague asked me to run for union office. I just wanted to do my job without abuse. And in the end, it wasn't me who was fired. I arrived at work one day and the newsroom was abuzz with the news that Ralph Restak was suddenly no longer working at the *Star Tribune*. Soon afterward I stopped in to see the HR director, a very nice man, and he beamed when he saw me.

But by that time I was pretty worn down both physically and mentally. I continued to work for several months, but I knew it was coming to an end. When I discovered that I could start Social Security at age sixty-two, my opportunity had come, and I decided to retire.

I had stayed years longer than I should have because I wanted to retire on my own terms. I shunned the usual newsroom party where people get up and tell you how wonderful you are. It wasn't my style. It was hard to leave my many friends, especially Jim and Karen, with whom I'd spent so much time in the trenches (where, fortunately, margaritas were available.)

I left the *Strib* physically broken, but still with a little of the resilience that had powered my entire life. I loved being a reporter. It was a great adventure in many ways. It would take two years after retirement to regain my mental equilibrium, but I was grateful to the *Strib* for giving me opportunities to write stories that were important to me as a journalist and as a woman, and for not putting me out to pasture when I became ill.

Despite not being good enough, despite facing so many obstacles to breaking into the profession, despite having to bounce back from illness so many times, the shy girl from Peterson was happy to be able to experience the joys of journalism in her native Minnesota.

51. I left the *Strib* physically broken, but still with a little of the resilience that had powered my entire life. I loved being a reporter. It was a great adventure in many ways.

52. A wonderful photo of Jon.

53. Our escapes also took us to Spain, Italy, Ireland, France, Scotland, Wales, Belgium, the Netherlands, and the Czech Republic. In the U.S. San Francisco was our special place. For instant affinity and conviviality, there is one place: Ireland. We went four times.

Chapter 29

D arcy was ten years old when we moved to Maine in 1977. After we moved back to Minnesota in 1989 she tried out the Twin Cities for a little while, but she could not get used to living in an area with six-lane freeways and 3.5 million people. And it was just too far from her friends. She had become a Mainer, and with a vengeance, so she decided to stay in Portland.

After I left the *Star Tribune*, and Jon and I decided it was time to retire, it was not hard to decide that returning to Portland, and Darcy, was what we wanted to do, and so we did, in the spring of 2007. It was good seeing her regularly after so many years apart. We went to garage sales and political events, made strawberry jam and cursed Republicans. I knew what I was getting into when I went out and about with her. She knew *everyone*, so inevitably she ran into an acquaintance and indulged her penchant for chatting. "Sorry about that," she would say afterward. "That was so and so. She's a good Democrat." Jon and I, introverted Norwegian parents, never did solve the Mystery of the Gregarious Daughter.

Our new lives in Portland promised to be simpler: just one area code, one freeway, and a sign at the border saying, "Welcome to Maine: the way life should be." We began to resettle into a strange land with wicked funny accents; Moxie, a molasses-tasting soft drink; fiddleheads, think eating ferns; Whoopie Pies, with a gut-disturbing shortening-like filling; and strange fish, though not nearly as strange as lutefisk. Darcy had survived this exotica, and we would, too.

Maine has beauty beyond measure—the triple joy of lakes, mountains, and an ocean, starlit nights without light pollution. Portland is an urban area with thousands, not millions, of people, and uncommon riches in the arts and civic life. It is a smaller world than the one we left in the Twin Cities. One day early on a horn honked and the driver asked, "Are you still living in Minnesota?" It was the former district attorney. And a volunteer at a church sale asked, "Did you use to work at the paper?" It was the South Portland city attorney. This, nearly twenty years after I covered courts for the Portland papers. Small world indeed.

On the fifth day after we arrived we found a house in South Portland, high on a hill above Portland harbor. Our decision soon shouted out to us, "Yes! Absolutely, yes!" Meeting House Hill is a leafy old neighborhood close to all the amenities. The 1922 house had good bones and had been thoroughly renovated, so I had nothing to do but paint. Then I retreated to my yard with its multiple garden spaces. On the day we left Minnesota I stuffed cuttings of my mother's lilacs and rhubarb into the car with Jon shouting, "Stop! Stop! The car is full." Now these growing things with their sentimental attachments became harbingers of our new life.

In the garden I have the pleasures of watching blooms appear, then give way to others as the summer sun marches across the sky to the inevitability of cold and snow. They provide pleasure to others, too. "I come by your house with my grandson nearly every day so I can see your flowers," said one passerby. I had to give up on my veggie garden after some bad-tomato years. What's the point of all that effort if you can't eat fresh tomatoes for lunch every day?

Jon took to rewarding pursuits, tutoring African refugees in English and the citizenship exam. He took up cooking, read voraciously, practiced his Spanish, and studied the baseball box scores. We golfed, watched the Minnesota Twins, listened to Jane Austen on tape, cooked adventurously, and looked after each other. Every once in a while he'd say, "Don't we live in a great place?"

Chapter 30

I t was our search for the perfect beer. We became beer aficionados in our travels, and it was on our first trip to England that we discovered "real ale," the country's national drink. On our second, we discovered some special pubs and beers. On our third, we got serious. We based ourselves in London but made forays into the countryside, where there were thousands of pubs and hundreds of real ales waiting to be savored.

Our guide was "The Best Pubs of Great Britain," put out by the Campaign for Real Ale (CAMRA), an amazing grass roots organization that managed to halt a movement toward the introduction of taste-free American-style beers, a la Miller and Budweiser.

We tasted Robinwood Brewery's Old Fart at the Tap & Spile, just outside the walled City of York (where we visited a Viking village preserved underground.) We savored Timothy Taylor's Ram Tam in Howarth, just down the street from the Brontë parsonage. We sipped Old Peculier at Tweedie's in Grasmere, not far from William Wordsworth's house.

"The first fifty or sixty beers were easy—it took only a few weeks to reach that many," Jon, the list keeper, wrote to friends. "The final twenty or so were a struggle. It was hard, thirsty work, but someone had to do it."

The beer drinkers who banded together in CAMRA knew what they wanted: traditional, cask-conditioned ales that they had become accustomed to drinking in their local pubs. It was beer brewed without preservatives, delivered to pub cellars to continue the fermentation process, served without the artificial fizz of carbonation. They didn't want highly processed beers with a shelf life from here to eternity. Real ales are mellow and soothing, perfect for leisurely pub drinking.

The CAMRA folks knew what they were up against. A handful of big brewers owned a large chunk of England's pubs and generally served only their own beers in them. But CAMRA was so successful that the large brewers began brewing their own quality real ales as well as serving "guest" beers in their pubs. "It is," columnist Simon Jenkins wrote in *The Times* of London, "one of the consumer triumphs of our age."

None of these beers are intended to be swilled. They are to be sipped slowly in the conviviality of a pub. That was the plus of searching for the perfect beer: We found some great pubs. Our favorite was the Holly Bush near our Hampstead flat. It wasn't as old as the thirteenth century Turf Tavern in Oxford, which was so low-ceilinged that it had a sign on a rafter, "Mind your head." It wasn't as tiny as the Nags Head in Belgravia which had a cozy, neighborhood feel despite being in the heart of London. It wasn't picturesquely rural like the Falkland Arms, a thatch-roofed seventeenth century pub in the tiny Cotswold village of Great Tew. But the Holly Bush was old enough to have character—it hadn't been gussied up. In the early days it had a bonus: a barman named Michael, who served us lunches of meat pies and other hearty English food that kept us going all day.

Sometimes it was difficult for us to figure out whether we liked a pub for its beers and its aesthetics or for the people we met and the good time we had there. At The Cloisters in Salisbury we met Steve, an unemployed carpenter who approached us by saying, "Excuse me, but are you colonials?" To which Jon replied, "Better than involuntary Australians." Steve clearly was looking for someone to entertain, and we were it. He did entertain us—for four hours!—with a wit honed in his native Cornwall.

In Sheffield we found new English friends. They squired us around to places such as the Frog & Parrot, where we sampled what the pub proudly advertised as "the world's strongest draft beer," Roger & Out, gravity 1.125 (which is off the charts!) It is served only in one-third pints, and you get a certificate for drinking one. It was far too sweet and thick for our liking.

There were hits and misses, but it was serious pleasure, this search for the perfect beer. When we returned home, we had compiled a list of seventy-eight beers, alphabetized and ranked by quality. What was the perfect beer? Bishop's Tipple came close. So did Wobbly Bob. But we had a hunch it was still out there. The search continued.

§

Walking down a London street on a sunny September afternoon I was feeling carefree and blessed. I was here with Jon, my whimsical and worldly-wise travel companion, in a place that was special to both of us. I was on my way to meet Jon at the Museum Tavern, where we would have a couple of our favorite ales and some classic British food before heading off to a play.

I was inside my head when a voice brought me out of my reverie, "Excuse me, can you direct me to Russell Square?"

"Of course," I said. "Go to the end of this long block and turn left and you'll be right there." I felt a grin mosey over my face. He thought I was a local!

At the Museum Tavern, Jon, a die-hard Anglophile and aficionado of British theater, is having his own adventure. He's sitting there having a pint of Abbot Ale when a booming voice pierces the quiet of the nearly empty pub, "A pound seventeen for a bottle of beer! You've got to be mad!" It is one of the most distinctive voices in all of British theater, spoken by Sir John Hurt, a renowned actor who in later life played the wand shop owner Ollivander in the Harry Potter movies.

Jon strikes up a conversation with him, saying how much he liked Hurt's performance in the movie "1984." They talk about George Orwell, one of Jon's heroes, and the injustices of life. Hurt asks Jon if he's in London on an "emotional" or "academic" escape. "Just taking a break," Jon said. "Sounds like an emotional escape," Hurt said. "I'm convinced that everything in life is an escape."

London was our favorite escape, a place for once-shy Midwesterners to spread our wings. We could hate England's colonial hegemony but still love London, which embraced us as we embraced it. It is full of stories, full of surprises. After a bad experience asking for directions from a New York City cop— "What do you think I am, a ****ing tour guide?"—we decided to test a London bobby. Jon asked him for directions to the place where we were standing, as if we didn't know where we were. His response, "What luck, sir! You're here!"

On one visit, London seemed to be mired in social confusion. Many Londoners were wearing black, and punks were in vogue, wearing chains and leather jackets with their hair in long green spikes that looked like lethal weapons. Because they were so out front, I figured they wouldn't mind one wee tourist taking one wee photo. Wrong. When my subject heard my camera click as I photographed her from behind, she wheeled around, grabbed my arm and promised assorted mayhem if I did it again. I didn't do it again, but I did get my picture.

Theater was our special passion. On every London trip we saw several plays, with Jon setting off each morning for the half-price ticket booth where good seats were usually available at a discount. We saw some of the most renowned actors in British theater, starting with Vanessa Redgrave, Natasha Richardson, and Jonathan Pryce in "The Seagull." Other favorites were Alec Guinness and Edward Herman in "A Walk in the Woods"; "A Room of One's Own," a one-woman show starring Eileen Atkins as Virginia Woolf, my personal favorite; "An Inspector Calls," a classic by J.B. Priestley; Michael Frayn's "Noises off," the funniest by far; and "The History Boys," our favorite of the dozens we saw over the years.

§

Our escapes also took us to Spain, Italy, Ireland, France, Scotland, Wales, Belgium, the Netherlands, and the Czech Republic. In the U.S. San Francisco was our special place.

For instant affinity and conviviality, there is one place: Ireland. We went four times. I figured out early on that you don't rebuff an Irishman—it's rude. If he stops you on the street and wants to talk, you talk. If he wants to take you to a pub, you go. You can count on good craic, as the Irish say—i.e., a fine time.

Even Irish children don't like to be rebuffed. One Sunday in Limerick we came across a group of panhandling children straight out of Mass. When Jon rejected their requests for "a little something," one girl, disgusted with him but apparently still wanting to be polite, said "Aw, go on with you, please."

Besides charm and wit, kindness and generosity are in the Irish DNA. One late night in Dublin we were the only people on a bus when the driver asked us where we were going. He went out of his way to take us directly to our B&B.

Another time, when we went to see a terrific band—Hank Halfhead and the Rambling Turkeys—the band leader invited us to the band's gig the following night at the Trinity College Law School. "Just ask for me," he said. Exciting! But when we opened the doors and saw all the law students in tuxes and ball gowns, we of the backpacks and jeans decided we would not go in.

Being an American on the streets of Dublin, especially late at night and lost, makes you a magnet. We remember only one episode that didn't end well. A medical student let us in the back door of a closed pub and introduced us to his friends. When we told them we were going to the North the next day to visit friends, they said they weren't going to tell us about the border crossing, the demarcation line between the Republic and the North: "Let's let them experience it for themselves." They seemed to be having fun with us.

This was during the Troubles, and crossing the border was neither fun nor funny. A soldier who looked about eighteen kept his rifle trained on us from just a few feet away as his compatriot asked for Jon's license. I stopped breathing. I didn't dare move a finger. When the compatriot cleared us to resume our trip, at least he wished us "a good holiday."

On one trip we drove around the Ring of Kerry, a thirty-mile trip with striking views, to Dingle, where we settled into Mrs. Leonard's B&B. We then headed off to O'Flaherty's, Dingle's premier traditional music pub, for which the word "gritty" was coined. A mangy but lovable dog gave up his spot to us on a cushioned bench with the stuffing falling out. The pub deserved its musical billing. We stayed until closing, then headed back to Mrs. Leonard's, where we found hot water bottles in our bed.

I had flown over not feeling very well, but since our arrival the discomfort in my chest had turned to pain. The next day, a Saturday, Mrs. Leonard sent us down the street to see Dr. Fanning, who gave me meds to tide me over on the hour-long drive to Tralee. There I went into a 1940s-era Catholic hospital for an X-ray and saw Dr.

O'Regan, who had stayed late on a Saturday to see me. He was gracious and welcoming. When he wondered why I didn't scream in pain when he thumped me on my chest, I said, "I'm Nordic." Then he told us about his visit to the Norwegian pavilion at Disney World. He gave me strong meds, and we checked into a hotel so I could take hot baths regularly. In a few days I was well, and we were on the road again.

Traveling with Jon was always educational, as was life with Jon for fifty-three years. One of his former bosses once said to me, "So it's been one continuous seminar, has it?" But the classes were suspended—temporarily—in Ireland. It was an astonishing moment. We were in a pub with a quiz show on a television behind us, and Jon was explaining the questions and answers, because I couldn't hear the TV. When he told me the answer to a question about a city where the streets are filled with water, I'd had it.

"I ain't playing this Eliza Doolittle game anymore," I said. When we both stopped laughing, he said, "That was terrific. What a great putdown." He allowed as how he had 'enry 'igginsed me to death over the years. But he was a scholar in many genres, and he couldn't bring himself to stop sharing his discoveries, and soon I resumed my role as student.

§

It wasn't all pubs and theater for us. We heard lots of music, usually in folk clubs, took walking tours, and visited every bookstore we came across, buying dozens of books we couldn't get in the U.S. One morning I awoke in a hotel room in Paris to find a note from Jon, "I love my wife, my wife of thirty-two years. I must buy her something here. Balzac?"

In Seville, Spain we saw a performance of flamenco dancing on the patio of an old palace that was electrifying. Jon said it was like going to your first-ever rock concert and seeing a guy named Springsteen.

In Madrid we discovered the *chocolaterías*, where you can drink chocolate straight up, then stagger out on a chocolate high. But it was the magnificent Prado Museum that drew us to the city. As Jon described his response to the Prado:

Limited as I am in knowledge of and feeling for art, I've never had the experience of being knocked out. Impressed? Touched? Fascinated? Yes. When you come upon Goya's *The Third of May, 1808* at the Prado, with one's head full of Titian, Velasquez, and Rubens, it deals a knockout blow.

We compiled a thick binder on each of our trips, assembling the pieces of adventure, discovery, history, comedy, mishaps, which combine to create a well-traveled life. But behind these snippets there is a big picture, as described by Jon one morning in Barcelona:

> Donna was sleeping, so I went out to get coffee for both of us and soon found myself on the Ramblas on a golden, sunny, perfect Mediterranean morning. I experienced that on our first trip to Barca and long before that in London and Paris, that indefinable thrill you feel when you're in an amazing, beautiful city on a beautiful day, and you're just glad to be alive, to experience this.

54. Jon struck up a conversation with famed actor John Hurt in a pub. Hurt asks if Jon is in London on an emotional or academic escape. Just a break, Jon said. "Sounds like an emotional escape," Hurt said. "I'm convinced everything in life is an escape."

55. Me and Darcy in Ireland. Irish children don't like to be rebuffed. One Sunday in Limerick we came across a group of panhandling children straight out of Mass. When Jon rejected their requests for "a little something," one girl, disgusted with him but apparently still wanting to be polite, said "Aw, go on with you, please."

56. On our search for the perfect beer, we became beer aficionados, and it was on our first trip to England that we discovered "real ale," the country's national drink. On our second, we discovered some special pubs and beers. On our third, we got serious. We based ourselves in London but made forays into the countryside, where there were thousands of pubs and hundreds of real ales waiting to be savored.

Chapter 31

hen Jon was diagnosed with leukemia in February 2020, he had already battled multiple myeloma. His doctor said she hoped to give him "two good years." But the new cancer was brutal, and he died on May 13, 2020, at age seventy-four.

Darcy wrote on Facebook, "My beloved father, Jon Halvorsen, lost his valiant battle to acute leukemia and multiple myeloma this morning. My mother and I were at his side as he took his last breath. He was a retired journalist, world traveler, gourmet cook, and a scholar of all genres. My mother and I will miss him every day for the rest of our lives. Love you very much, Dad." It generated 255 comments the first day. More would come in from as far away as Africa and Europe in the days ahead.

Jon was born in Minneapolis to Ellen Edgar Halvorsen on September 7, 1945, and grew up there with a sister, Judy. His father, Ted, was in the Navy in the Panama Canal Zone when his son was born. Ted was nearly forty, and he was ready for this child. "Even when I was at my most annoying, he would explain things to me with a seemingly inexhaustible supply of patience," Jon said after his father died. "After all, he was a teacher for forty years."

"Most of all," Jon recalled, "Dad showed me what love looks like. It came shining through in his devotion to his grandchildren." And through his mother's eyes as she sat at the kitchen table with Jon for hours, listening, helping him find his way. He came to learn that "if you felt loved and approved of as a child, that's really all you need for a good start in life."

So it was that Jon brought to his life grace, patience, compassion, and love that he showered not only on his family, but also on the refugees he tutored at McDonald's in Portland on Sunday mornings; the foreign journalists whom we hosted at the World Press Institute in St. Paul; the children he cared for in a YWCA program; the Portland *Press Herald* colleagues he stood up for when their livelihoods were threatened; and the many journalists he mentored.

"You couldn't find another editor or friend who would stand up so readily for what was right," said Sharon Matzek, whom Jon supported when she and Mary Snell were seeking equal pay at the *Press Herald*. "He suffered professionally because he sided with us." *Press Herald* Reporter Bob Keyes said Jon guided him to a feature writing career by giving him an important assignment in his last week as a summer intern. After Jon died, Keyes said he would work with interns more enthusiastically "because of Jon's memory and to honor him."

Jon graduated from Washburn High School in Minneapolis, then went to the University of Minnesota to get a degree in journalism. There he met me, another student pursuing a career in newspapers, and we were married in my hometown of Peterson, Minnesota. After several pit stops around the country, our little family landed in Portland—finally getting it right—in the late 1970s. It struck both Jon and me as a magical place, and it felt like a final stop. We both worked for the Portland papers. I covered courts; Jon was the editor of *Audience*.

In Portland we discovered the camaraderie of coed softball games; in fact Jon was "the commissioner," who pleaded with his new friends to come to Fort Williams to play ball. We played winter "snowball" games with a ball I painted orange, and with a pot of whiskey warming in the dugout.

There were other games to be played, too. While Jon was easygoing, "he was also a fine athlete, an avid sports fan and really quite competitive," said his longtime tennis buddy, Doug Warren. The competitiveness extended to the dining room table where the two played a statistics-driven baseball board game called APBA. "When we found out we both grew up loving APBA, it really cemented our friendship." Doug said. "Jon was my kind of crazy."

As the editor of *Audience*, Jon covered Portland Stage, igniting an interest that led us to see sixty-five plays in London over the years. He often wrote about Schooner Fare, the legendary folk band whose music etched Maine on our souls. "He made us all better people for having known him," said band member Steve Romanoff.

Strife at the newspaper eventually prompted us to return to Minnesota, where my family lived. Jon became Managing Editor of the Macalester College alumni magazine and I became a reporter for the Minneapolis *Star Tribune*. While there, sadly, all four of our parents died in a two-year period.

We found consolation in my family, new friends and the ten journalists from eight countries we hosted through WPI. Cordelia Onu of Nigeria wondered, when she was chosen in 1999, why she needed "parents." "I was a mother of three, and I did not see why I would be needing parents," she recalled. But she relented and "became a child once again in an American home." She wrote to me after Jon's death, "The host parents stick to you for life. I salute them and the spirit of Jon Halvorsen. He was a great man. He loved and served his country and showcased true Americaness. May heaven receive his soul and give him a just reward and rest."

While Jon's career path was in journalism, he was ultimately a teacher. "If you're really, really lucky, maybe once in your life you'll work for someone like Jon Halvorsen," said Jan Shaw-Flamm, longtime Macalester writer. "He cultivated us and taught us with the sort of thoughtful and kind critique that made you burn to dig in, understand more, and write to a higher standard because he knew you were capable of it."

With his leukemia diagnosis, Jon's learning was slowed but not entirely stopped. He continued to order used books from independent bookstores around the country. As always, he would smell the pages. They were like a tonic. His tutoring was like a tonic to him, too. One student's new citizenship allowed him to visit his children in Somalia for the first time in fifteen years. "I am so sorry, my heart is sad," he wrote after learning of Jon's death. "I hope he is helping angels."

57. Jon's departure from Macalester.

58. Jon took to rewarding pursuits, tutoring African refugees in English and the citizenship exam. He took up cooking, read voraciously, practiced his Spanish, and studied the baseball box scores. We golfed, watched the Minnesota Twins, listened to Jane Austen on tape, cooked adventurously, and looked after each other.

Chapter 32

M y emigrant family's 1869 home, two rooms, a loft and a small entryway held up by rocks, is tucked into a birch-studded hillside. In the old, faded photograph I hold in my hands livestock graze close to the house, where stacks of grain also stand ready to feed them. Off to the side are two wood-framed outbuildings. It is an arresting image of primitive pioneer circumstances.

The house was smaller than many Norwegian-built homes in the area, but Thor Kittelsen and Gunhild Nielsdatter had only one child, our grandfather, Charley, when they arrived in Minnesota. We don't know why they came, though they didn't seem destitute. Unlike many Norwegian immigrants, who came to this country with a dream of owning their own land, great-grandfather Thor Kittelsen owned his own land as a *gaardbruger selveier*, the highest class of land ownership in Norway. The farm, handed down through his family since the 1700s, was simple: he had two cows, four sheep, a quarter acre of barley, half an acre of oats, and three acres of potatoes.

He sold half of the farm six years earlier, and at thirty-one he used some of the proceeds to book passage to America on the Monsoon, a three-masted sailing ship (built in Bath, Maine!) carrying eighty-eight passengers, a more comfortable ship than most Norwegian emigrants could afford. Together with his family—his wife Gunhild, their seven-year-old son Kittel (our grandfather Charley) and baby Niels, nine months old—they set sail from the southeastern port of Kragero at the beginning of April 1869, and after six weeks at sea they arrived in Quebec on May 14.

To reach southern Minnesota they still had to cross half the continent—1,500 miles—at a time when railroad construction was just beginning. It was a difficult and expensive journey; perhaps they got help from Norwegian settlers along the way. Baby Niels did not survive the trip, but there is no record of what happened to him. He could have died on the ship or on the arduous overland journey.

Their destination was Fillmore County, which for many Norwegians was the Promised Land, and where, one promoter proclaimed, the soil was "warm and quick, naturally of fine tilth … is ready made, needs no manuring, and is almost a stranger to weeds." They began the arduous process of starting over, building a homestead, buying livestock, and planting crops. Two years later another son was born, and he too was given the name of Niels.

I look at the photo, taken by my grandfather Charley, of his parents and his younger brother Niels—by now a young man—and I wonder what life was like for them. They had changed the family name from Kittelsen to Hasleiet after the name of the farm in Norway they had sold to start this new life. Though their circumstances might have seemed primitive, they were not alone in this new world. In coming to Fillmore County, they had settled among their own people.

In 1850, when it was still a territory, there were only nine Norwegians living in Minnesota. Twenty years later there were nearly 50,000, and many of them had settled in Fillmore County. The rapid growth was spurred by the end of the Civil War, which had frightened off many would-be Norwegian emigrants, the free land that was available under the Homestead Act, and new lands opening up as the Indian Wars were winding down—a sickening chapter in our history, from which we and other whites reaped the benefits. A few months after the Hasleiets arrived, Norwegian journalist Svein Nilssen wrote about southern Minnesota, "A newcomer from Norway who arrives here will be surprised indeed to find in the heart of the country, more than a thousand miles from his landing place, a town where language and way of life so unmistakably remind him of his native land."

They named their homestead Diamond Creek after the stream that ran through it—a beautiful name for a beautiful and idyllic spot, but in truth it was 160 acres cobbled together from what was left over after earlier settlers had claimed the vast expanses of richer, tillable land on the plateau above their valley. It was isolated, hemmed in by hills with no other houses in sight, and a dirt road to get to civilization.

They made a life of it, though it was hard and marred by tragedy. Niels, Charley's only brother, died of tuberculosis at age thirty-two, as did their father, Thor, eight years later at age seventy-two. Thor and Niels were still alive when Charley built a house for himself and his new family on the other side of Diamond Creek in 1899. But his mother, Gunhild, had died five years earlier at sixty-one, cause unknown. In that tiny three-room house Charley and his wife Mary raised their eight children, my dad, Alfred, the youngest of them.

In their wedding photo Charley is a big guy sitting on a chair while his tiny bride stands alongside him. People didn't smile in photos back then. Mary looks unusually stoic, knowing her first child is on the way and not knowing, as one of fourteen children herself, how many more will follow. A photo of an older Charley shows him sitting on the porch wearing a dapper suit and hat and throwing back his head in laughter. This photo, together with the stories Dad told me, create an image of my grandfather as an engaging guy with an adventurous spirit, unlike the taciturn Norwegians who filled my early history.

All four branches of my family came from Norway. All settled in Fillmore County and became farmers. Mary's parents settled in northern Iowa in 1862 and moved to Pilot Mound, Minnesota, in 1868. On my mother's side, her mother's family, the McCallsons, arrived in 1860, and her father's family, the Johnsons in 1865.

It was my father's side, the Hasleiets, I know the best. Grandpa Charley must have had a bit of money, perhaps saved during his years of working in Wisconsin—a period we know nothing about. He had one of the first cars in the area, bought musical instruments so the family could play together on cold winter nights, bought a fancy camera and rigged up a darkroom behind the house. Charley probably built such a tiny house for himself and Mary because he couldn't imagine—having only one brother who survived to adulthood—that he would have eight children.

Charley's photos of his family's farm and those surrounding, taken in his early twenties, give us an extraordinary view of Norwegian immigrant life in the 1880s. Decades later, in his eighties, shortly before he died he took the only photos of my family when we lived in Diamond Creek.

My Dad's sister, Emma Thompson, lived fifteen years longer than he did, and she was happy to tell me stories of the early days, until she died at ninety-six. From Emma's stories, from Charley's pictures, and from stories my dad told me, we can piece together a vision of their life in the first half of the twentieth century.

The family was nearly self-sufficient, as families had to be back then. They had pigs and chickens, laying hens for eggs, cows for milk and cream. They made butter in a wooden churn. They had a huge garden in which they grew every vegetable imaginable. In the fall, the family bought flour, sugar, coffee, and other staples to last until spring. In winter they stored vegetables and meat in a dirt cellar under the house.

They grew alfalfa for the livestock, but their only cash crop was tobacco. It seemed an unusual crop to grow so far north, but it was grown by hundreds of Norwegian farmers after it was brought to Minnesota by Yankees from the east. The Hasleiet kids helped with the crop, as they did with nearly every job on the farm. They helped plant tobacco seed from a horse-drawn rig, speared the tobacco leaves and hung them to dry on racks in the tobacco shed, and later picked off the dry leaves and packed them in boxes to be sold in La Crosse.

It was an idyllic life for the kids, but a hard life for Mary. Between ages twenty-two and thirty-seven she bore eight children and was responsible for every aspect of their lives until they were old enough to help out. Jon, my half-Norwegian husband, used to say that I wear him out with my Norwegian work ethic, but I can't imagine working as hard as Mary did. "Both emotionally and physically, pioneer life exacted the greatest toll on women," Norwegian historian Odd Lovoll wrote in *The Promise of America*.

She made clothes for the whole family until the girls were old enough to make their own. Even in the frigid Minnesota winters the girls wore dresses. They washed clothes in a big metal tub, carrying water from a pump just outside the door and heating it on the big cast iron kitchen stove. "We had to boil the white clothes," Emma remembers. "They were as white as snow. In the winter we washed them in the summer kitchen"—a one-room building near the house. "We hung them out until they froze. It didn't take too long for them to dry. They smelled so fresh when you took them in.

"My mother baked bread every day. We had a lot of plum sauce, a lot of jams and jellies, gooseberries and apples. We had an orchard on top of the hill … There were too many of us to have bacon and eggs for breakfast. We had big boxes of cereal, corn flakes, mostly. We had oatmeal quite a bit, too. My dad loved oatmeal." Mary also made lefse, the soft Norwegian flatbread made with potatoes that was a staple of the Norwegian diet. And, of course, she made lutefisk, the stinky Norwegian dish made from codfish preserved in lye that none of us children ever learned to like.

At Christmas the family went into the woods to cut down a tree, then put candles on it. They had chicken or turkey, potatoes, and corn for their holiday meal. The children each received one gift and candy.

Each morning the children walked to the one-room Diamond Creek school, about a mile away, along with other Norwegian kids, including the Hoffs, the Olsons, the Engebretsons, and the Hjelles. During recess they went outside to play ball in the pasture. If it was really cold, they stayed inside.

On summer weekends neighbors came to visit, and the kids played ball and swam in the swimming hole below the house. Mary's relatives came too, and she always fed whatever guests might arrive. In winter the kids went to neighbors' houses to play cards. Emma recalled getting lost in the hills one snowy night trying to find their way home.

When the winter snows came, Charley plowed the road with two of the family's three horses. On Sundays he drove the family—as many kids as would fit—to the Highland Church in a horse-drawn buggy. Emma remembers when he got that first car: "He stepped on the foot feed, and when the car took off, he said, 'Whoa, whoa, whoa!' The car stopped before he hit anything. He didn't do much driving. Once the boys were older, they drove him."

Emma remembers with fondness the family's musical evenings. I don't know how they got an organ into that tiny house but somehow they did. Emma chorded the organ, while Dad played the guitar and Charley the fiddle. Charley definitely had musical genes; he could play the guitar and accordion, too, and my dad inherited those genes.

Thor and Gunhild Hasleiet's original homestead is long gone now, but we know what it looked like because of Charley's photos.

They came a long distance to settle in this remote corner of pioneer America, but together with their neighbors they managed to bring a big piece of Norway with them. No matter why they came, I'm glad they did. This historic place is where my life began seventy-five years after their arrival.

59. My emigrant family's 1869 home, two rooms, a loft and a small entryway held up by rocks, is tucked into a birch-studded hillside. In the old, faded photograph I hold in my hands livestock graze close to the house, where stacks of grain also stand ready to feed them. Off to the side are two wood-framed outbuildings. It is an arresting image of primitive pioneer circumstances.

60. My Dad's sister, Emma Thompson, lived fifteen years longer than he did, and she was happy to tell me stories of the early days, until she died at ninety-six. It was an idyllic life for the kids, but a hard life for Great grandma Mary. Between ages twenty-two and thirty-seven she bore eight children and was responsible for every aspect of their lives until they were old enough to help out. Jon used to say that I wear him out with my Norwegian work ethic, but I can't imagine working as hard as Mary did. "Both emotionally and physically, pioneer life exacted the greatest toll on women," Norwegian historian Odd Lovoll wrote in *The Promise of America*.

Chapter 33

J on's job at Macalester College opened the door to my first trip to Norway. It was unexpected for both of us.

When the Nobel Peace Prize was awarded to Kofi Annan, Secretary General of the United Nations along with the U.N. itself, Jon was asked to cover it. Annan was a graduate of Macalester and Jon was Managing Editor of the alumni magazine. Of course, I wanted to accompany him, and the *Strib* said I could cover it if I paid my own airfare.

The thing about heroes is that you can't always tell who will become one. Annan is a slight, soft-spoken man from Ghana, who might have seemed unlikely to ascend to this pinnacle of success on the world stage. But Annan's Macalester classmates and professors were certain he was destined for great things. They were not surprised that he would enter the majestic Oslo City Hall to the flourish of trumpets and the applause of a thousand people.

Jon and I sat in the audience at the Nobel concert, attended by 6,000 people, where the world-class performers included Paul McCartney, Youssou N'Dour, Wyclef Jean, and Barbara Hendricks. On stage, Meryl Streep asked Annan what effect receiving the Nobel would have on the U.N. and on him. He replied, "Maybe you will pay a little more attention when we say something now."

Gunnar Berge, Chairman of the Norwegian Nobel Committee, said Annan gave the United Nations "external prestige and inner morale the likes of which the organization had hardly seen in its fifty-year history."

In his remarks, Annan narrowed the conversation down to preserving the humanity of individuals, saying the world needs to care as much about a baby girl in Afghanistan as it does about achieving peace among warring nations. "We must focus as never before on improving the condition of the individual men and women who give the state or nation its richness and character," he said. "We must begin with a girl in Afghanistan, recognizing that saving that one life is to save humanity itself."

In remarks that may seem quixotic all these years later, given the wanton violation of human dignity all over the world, he said:

> A genocide begins with the killing of one man, not for what he has done but because of who he is … A campaign of ethnic cleansing begins with one neighbor turning on another … What begins with the failure to uphold the dignity of one life all too often ends up with a calamity for entire nations.

It was a quick but rewarding trip for Jon and me. We were impressed by our mother country's sturdy character and the friendliness of its people. We felt pride when people spoke to us in Norwegian—we look like them, don't we? When we told them we didn't speak the language, they spoke to us in perfect English.

We went to the Resistance Museum, which tells the story of Norway's resistance during Nazi Germany's occupation from 1940 to 1945. Jon and I were always proud of that story, which we thought demonstrated a national strength of character.

We went to the famous cafe and bakery Halvorsens Conditori—an Oslo institution—for coffee and pastries, to Engebret Cafe, Oslo's oldest restaurant, for medallions of reindeer with port and raisin sauce, and to lunch at the Grand Cafe, where playwright Henrik Ibsen and painter Edvard Munch, giants of Norwegian culture, had regular tables. We photographed a statue of Johan Halvorsen, Norway's most famed composer and violinist, for the name, of course.

While there, Jon received an email from a colleague, "Are you and Donna basking in Norwegian glory? Are you mixing it up with the world's beautiful people?" We didn't have time to "mix it up," but we were grateful for this delightful trip. We experienced the craziness of winter days in which the sun peeked over the horizon at 9:07 A.M. and disappeared at 3:12 P.M. After a while, these days of so little sunlight might have seemed an inconvenience to people like us, but in the end I decided I would trade the humanity of Norway for a little less sun.

When we returned home I started a Norwegian language class, but quit because I couldn't hear well enough to pick up the sounds. Two years later, language or no language, my sister Nancy and I were ready to go to Norway in search of our roots.

61. When the Nobel Peace Prize was awarded to Kofi Annan, Secretary General of the United Nations along with the U.N. itself, Jon was asked to cover it.

62. Hasleiet house, Norway.

✝

OLA BØTUN
✻ 1810 ✝ 1872

MARTA BØTUN
✻ 1805 ✝ 1886

JON BØTUN
✻ 1831 ✝ 1907

GYRID BØTUN
✻ 1849 ✝ 1914

BRITA ✻ 1870 ✝ 1884

TOR ✻ 1885 ✝ 1886

GJERTRUD BØTHUN
✻ 1877 ✝ 1940
ISAK BØTHUN
✻ 1874 ✝ 1963

63. Botun family gravesite.

180

Chapter 34

We were the only persons on the street when we left our Bergen lodgings that first day. The fish market was just setting up. The fishmonger yelled over at us, "Are you from Minnesota?"

We looked at each other, astounded, "How did you know?"

"Everybody who comes here is from Minnesota," he replied. We laughed, we Hasleiet girls from Minnesota. "Yes! We belong here."

Nancy and I had been interested in our family's story since the 1970s, but we didn't think about going to Norway in the early years because we had so little to go on. Relatives couldn't tell us much, and Norwegian pastors often couldn't help us.

Then came the Internet, which opened up a whole new world to researchers. Even then we were tripped up by similar names (so many Ole Olsens!), changing names (Kittelsen became Hasleiet, Peterson became Ramsey), and wildly different spellings (Hasleiet/Hasseleid, Ramsøy/Ramsey).

By the time we set off in May 2003, bearing our Norwegian married names, Halvorsen and Rustad, we were only marginally competent in genealogy. We didn't know if we would find any living relatives. But we felt we would be satisfied by just seeing the places where they lived. We just wanted to see those places and imagine what their lives were like in the 1800s, before they left their homeland behind.

We had always prided ourselves on being 100 percent Norwegian, but a shirttail relative had told us that our ancestors on the maternal grandfather Johnson's branch of the family included King Eric the Victorious of Sweden and his wife Sigrid the

Haughty; Rurik, the Swedish founder of Russia; plus a couple of Danish kings and a Greek princess—going back to the 800s. "Yah, sure, you betcha," we said. But when you stop to think about it, it would be difficult to be 100 percent anything, given ever-changing European boundaries and the perpetual wanderings of our Viking forebears—who left a legitimate mark on European history, along with the pitter patter of many little feet.

What we knew for sure was that our ancestors were Norwegian going back at least to the 1600s, and that was good enough for us. We knew that all of our great-grandparents left Norway in the 1850s and 1860s and had settled in northern Iowa and southern Minnesota.

We started out by looking for evidence of the Johnsons and the McCallsons on my mother's side of the family. We drove to Rennesoy on the west coast of Norway and after driving around in circles found ourselves taken in and assisted by a gracious man named Svein Ullenes, who was fascinated by the Norwegians who went to America and mesmerized by the loose-leaf binder of genealogy we carried that showed some names that matched his. Svein, who spoke no English, introduced us to the church pastor, who translated for us, and invited us to explore the church graveyard. But despite all of our efforts we were unable to locate the farms of either of the two branches of our mother's family.

§

Our trip from Oslo to Bergen took us by train through some of the most beautiful parts of Norway. The train stopped in the village of Flam, at the doorstep of one of our ancestral homes. We disembarked, walked up a slight hill and there it was: the name Ramsøy on a house. This was the farm we had been looking for, the home of Bottolf Peterson, the father of our grandmother Mary, Charley's wife. Some years after settling in America Bottolf would change his last name to the family's ancestral name, Ramsøy, with the English spelling, Ramsey. His wife Gjertrude took the name Julia Ramsey.

When no one responded to our knock we found a neighbor, Jøstein Buene, who said his friend Asbjørn Ramsøy was at work.

He called Asbjørn but he said he was sorry he couldn't see us—he would be heading out of town for the weekend directly from work. It was a missed opportunity but our journey was just beginning.

We knew from our research that Grandma Mary's parents, Bottolf Peterson and his wife Gjertrud Mikkelsdatter Botun, moved from the Ramsøy farm to nearby Leikanger in 1854, but we didn't know why. Could it be because their first child, Mikkel, was born out of wedlock that year, a shameful thing? Or maybe because the Ramsøy farm could not support all the people who lived on it?

Some Norwegian farms prospered, but many struggled. The Ramsøy farm was being squeezed as early as 1845, when the census showed sixty-two people living in three households on the farm. In 1866 alone, five percent of the population from the Sogn district in western Norway left for America.

Bottolf's father, Peter, and his sister, Marta, had emigrated to Washington Prairie, Iowa in 1856, and Bottolf and his family joined them six years later. Bottolf and his wife would have thirteen more children, the last of them in Pilot Mound, Minnesota, where they settled permanently in 1867. The youngest of the eight surviving children was our grandmother, Mary.

Two years after our visit, we were excited to hear that the area surrounding the Ramsøy farm was dedicated as a UNESCO World Heritage Site. UNESCO said that Nærøyfjord and Geirangerfjord "are considered to be among the most scenically outstanding fjord areas on the planet," as well as the least affected by human activity. In a UNESCO photo we can see the Ramsøy farm and the door we knocked on.

§

Every day we were thrilled by the stunning beauty of the land our great-grandparents had left behind when they came to Minnesota. But so far we had not succeeded in meeting any living relatives. Undeterred, we had high hopes when we set out to find the Botuns, the family of our great-grandmother, the mother of Mary Ramsey Hasleiet, Charley's wife. Though we were optimistic, we had no idea how severe our logistic challenges were. I had never traveled overseas without Jon, a master planner, and Nancy had never been abroad, although she was a good organizer and terribly commonsensical. I hoped she would counter my directional dyslexia, which means I instinctively go the wrong way, a terrible thing to inflict on a traveling companion.

We had been told that Norwegians were exceptionally friendly, and we could knock on any door at any time and get help. But there was no civilization in sight as we drove over a huge snowy mountain in search of the Botuns.

We obviously did not know how to read Norwegian maps. The mountain took us by surprise, as did the fifteen narrow, dimly lit tunnels I drove through on the way to the mountain. My poor depth perception (another malady) hit me with full force. It was my scariest driving ever. I didn't tell Nancy how scared I was. Nor did she, with a lifelong fear of heights, tell me the terror she felt when she drove over the Vikafjellet, the Vik Mountain. We both wondered, "Whose idea was this?" as we competed for the narrow, zigzagging road with eighteen-wheelers and the tour buses already on the road early in the season. There was snow as far as we could see. I tried not to look at Nancy's frozen face. I, the seasoned traveler, thought, "What have I done to her?"

At the top we drove between fifteen-foot snowbanks that stood straight up as if carved with a massive knife. We exhaled as we drove down the mountain to the town of Vik. It was the middle of May, and eating dinner in daylight at 10:00 P.M. was a momentary delight.

The next day I drove along a fjord to Fresvik, population 280 or so. Dad's grandmother was Gjertrud Botun and the Botun farm was the oldest in the village. We arrived on a national holiday, May 17, Syttende Mai, and Norwegians were gathering to celebrate the signing of their constitution. As we drove into the mountainside village we stopped alongside a beautifully costumed family and said, "We're looking for our family, the Botuns." They replied, "We're Botuns," so we took a photo of them.

We drove on to the school, where a parade was forming. A group of people soon gathered around us, eager to help. After the parade and ceremony, a woman who knew the village well took us to her home to look through records, but no luck. We went to the church, where the cemetery was loaded with Botuns, many buried on top of each other for generations. We were told that to conserve space in their tiny villages, Norwegians bury their dead in coffins made of easily decomposing wood so another body can be buried in the same grave in thirty years.

Frazzled by names and dates, we had to concede defeat. The family we photographed weren't "our" Botuns but came to symbolize our Syttende Mai visit to this village and the family we didn't find. We hadn't found the Botuns we came looking for, but we left happy to be in our ancestral land on this sunlit day, greeted by such welcoming people on Norway's most important and colorful holiday.

§

It had cost $930 for us to rent a roller skate-sized car for five days, but what the heck—it got us over the mountain without dying of oxygen deprivation or sheer terror. We quickly learned that everything is expensive in Norway. We loved beer, but after paying $12 for our first bottles in a restaurant, we had to strategize. We would buy beer in supermarkets. Food, too. We weren't on a culinary tour. Who needs cod with aquavit or wild boar with whortleberry sauce when you have hazelnut bars and pizza (a small one cost $25). We stuffed ourselves with the free breakfasts, as bed-and-breakfast travelers usually do—oatmeal and hearty bread, sometimes with meats and cheeses, we ate everything but the herring. We'd rather starve than eat that.

We spent hours researching our lost relatives at the Emigration Center in Stavanger, and gathered lots of information but made no discoveries. We were running out of time and had saved the best for last. We actually knew where the Hasleiet farm was, sort of, because our cousins Elaine Lea Nordlie and Evie Berekvam Korsten had found it a year earlier. We also knew the most about our Hasleiet relatives, and a Hasleiet house still stood in the woods of southeastern Minnesota.

Nancy and I took a bus from Skien to Stathelle, where the guys at the taxi stand seemed to be debating which of them spoke the best English, or whether we would leave a big enough tip, or whether any of them had a clue as to where we wanted to end up. Our driver clearly didn't know where he was going, but without him we'd still be looking. A $60 cab ride later, with one road seeming more primitive than the last, he drove down a long, winding road into a sun-dappled green valley with a house, a barn, and another small building. We wondered aloud whether we should ask the driver to wait. Could we really call a taxi from here and get one? Our burly, blond driver took offense, "I found it didn't I?" and we let him go.

Our family had owned this place from 1763 to 1869, when they'd sold it to Solveig Hasseleid's family. It is in her family still. The farm is called Hasseleidet. When cousin Elaine had recalled driving onto the farm a year earlier, she said, "It felt like we were driving into the valley where our relatives settled in Fillmore County."

Solveig Hasseleid was beaming when she came out to greet us, delighted to meet more Hasleiets. "My brother, Gunnar, thought it was fun to meet you—the descendants of Thor Kittelsen," she wrote to Elaine after her visit. She showed us a photo of her great-grandparents, who had bought the farm from our family. The house, modernized in 1899, was lovely and more substantial than the modest wood-framed house Charley built for Mary in Diamond Creek that same year, and no wonder—it had to be big enough for Solveig and her five brothers.

We chatted a while, then sat down to a table laden with luscious sweets and superb coffee. Solveig could speak little English, so her niece AnneLis translated our conversation. Another niece, Ingrid, and her son were also there.

We walked around the farm, which is located on an isthmus between Skjærsjø and Grummestad lakes. Amazingly, it didn't have a road for decades, if not centuries. "In summer we rowed across the lakes," Solveig said. "In the winter we walked across the lakes if the ice was thick enough. If it wasn't, we skied through the woods. When we walked, it took us an hour to get to school. We were used to walking, so we didn't mind. Now we have a road to the farm." That's the road our cabbie miraculously found.

Solveig showed us the tiny building that stood on the spot where the house of our relatives had once stood. The original house was so rotten that Solveig torn it down about seven years earlier and built a new one on its foundation, a single-room house with a gleaming hardwood floor and a sleeping loft. "You will stay here when you come back," she said.

Solveig's mother, Ingeborg, grew up on the farm and inherited it in 1935 when her father died. In those days they grew grain, potatoes, and other vegetables, though the farm was not large enough to support a family, so Solveig's grandfather worked at a sawmill and did field work for other farmers.

Solveig, who was born in 1925, worked as a nurse in the nearby town of Porsgrunn, where she had an apartment. But she had moved back to the farm to look after her brother Gunnar, who was newly blind. He had a guide dog, and she put up a rope fence from his house to hers so that he could get to her house on his own.

As we prepared to leave, Solveig wanted to feed us again. It was a Norwegian woman's gift of love that was familiar to us, but we were flying home from Oslo the next day. If we had planned better, we could have stayed in the little house Solveig had built on the foundation of our great-grandparents' house, as if to keep faith with our history.

AnneLis and Solveig drove us to the bus stop and stayed until the bus arrived. The Hasseleids weren't related to us but they sure felt like family. We didn't know if we'd ever see them again. Solveig was seventy-eight years old. But three weeks after we got home we were excited to hear that Solveig and AnneLis were coming to Minnesota for a visit in September.

64. Our visitors from Norway, from the left, AnneLis and Solveig, with our cousin Elaine Lea Nordlie.

65. The fishmonger yelled over at us, "Are you from Minnesota?" Nancy and I looked at each other, astounded, "How did you know?" He replied, "Everybody who comes here is from Minnesota," he replied. We laughed, we Hasleiet girls from Minnesota. "Yes! We belong here."

66. AnneLis and Solveig, visitors from Norway, join cousin Elaine Nordlie and the rest of the Hasleiet clan at Diamond Creek."

Chapter 35

T he place I call Diamond Creek, deep in the southeastern Minnesota hills, has such a hold on my soul. Long ago the property had become part of a state hardwood forest so it was no longer in the family. The state did not permit any major renovations but our cousins, the Berekvams of La Crosse, Wisconsin, leased the property and lovingly tended the place over the years. They maintained a park-like setting around the house that was so welcoming to the rest of us, and reunions were held there—a lovely spot in the woods, a respite for our extended family.

My siblings, Verdon, Wayne, Nancy, and I wanted to know what life was like for Thor and his little family, so, on one sunny fall afternoon we clambered across the creek seeking evidence of their lives. We dug in the foundation of the house but found only a couple of old forks, parts of a stove, and pieces of a brown jug that I took home and glued together.

One day when Aunt Emma Thompson, Dad's sister, and I drove to Diamond Creek, we saw a Hmong man cooking squirrel over a fire below the house. When we were leaving Emma said, "Drive down there. I want to talk to him." I wasn't sure this was a good idea. She rolled down her window and said, "This is my home place. Nice, isn't it?" The man nodded. She bore him no ill will, perhaps realizing that he was an immigrant, too.

Eventually, after I wrote to a local legislator telling him how important this historic property was to our family, the state relented and allowed us to paint and repair the house to keep it from falling into its dirt cellar. So it was, on a sunny Sunday in September, when Solveig and AnneLis came to visit us from Norway, that an army of cousins was "up in the valley" painting the house.

Solveig and AnneLis were so happy that we had kept the Hasleiet name—a name with a connection to the farm where their family has lived for 150 years—and they were impressed that we cared so much about our Norwegian heritage. Everything had to be translated for Solveig, so we didn't have time to tell our visitors long stories about Norwegian life on an American farm. But they understood that the house itself, now 120 years old, had many stories to tell.

I learned a lot about Diamond Creek from Dad. He loved the place, as I and my siblings do. After the family moved to Peterson, and whenever I returned for a visit after I moved away, we drove out there, sometimes just the two of us, winding along the rutted road perched at the edge of the bluff where gooseberries grew in summer. Once we found a hubcap from Charley's Model-T.

The house that Charley built had no electricity or running water, a pot-bellied stove for heat, and kerosene lamps for light. Wolves howled in the hills at night. When Dad was fourteen and his brother Alvin was seventeen, Alvin died of scarlet fever and a rattlesnake bite. Dad must have been lonely after that. His next oldest brother was twelve years older and long gone.

Dad adored his father for his adventurous spirit—and for his music. Using his father Thor's Norwegian fiddle, Charley used to gather the family together for musical evenings in front of the pot-bellied stove to take the chill off winter.

Eventually, when the rustic life became too hard for them, Dad's parents moved to Whalan, and my family moved into the Diamond Creek house. After work every day Dad would look in on them in their room in town. Dad was the youngest of the brood and the most responsible. Most of the others had moved away. Mary died when she was only sixty-seven. One month later, Dad found Charley dead too. He was eighty-five. I was two years old.

It was a huge loss to Dad. But he inherited—and passed on to his kids—his father's can-do spirit. He rode a motorcycle, took us to a motorcycle hill climb, to stock car races, even an Olympic ski trial. In later life, he taught himself to cook, to type, and to take pictures.

And just as it was for my Dad, the house that Charley built was the place where my brother Verdon and I spent our early childhoods, the fourth generation of our family to live on that land.

Though we were isolated, tucked into the hills, with no other houses in sight, I remember Mrs. Olson would yell from the top of the bluff when she needed a cup of sugar. It was the 1940s, but it was like growing up in the wilderness of a bygone era.

I remember being spanked for playing with matches and allegedly trying to set fire to the old house. In manly, little boy fashion, Verdon claimed he did it. We might have gone to the one-room Diamond Creek school that Dad and his siblings attended, but it had burned down. So when I was five we moved to Peterson—a move that brought major improvements in our lives: electricity, running water, and a bathroom.

My earliest memory of life in the house that Charley built was a ferocious afternoon storm that blackened the sky and sent water cascading down the hills through the yard and over the porch, taking our wooden rocking horse with it. Verdon and I clung to our mother as the house shook, the wind whistled, and the water roared as it pushed past the house. The foundation was not solid, so the house could have been swept away, but it stood.

67. Grandpa Charley and Grandma Mary. Wedding photo.

68. Grandpa Charley on the porch of the old homestead.

69. Winter at Diamond Creek.

Acknowledgments

Writing a book about yourself is not a Norwegian thing to do. It violates a central tenet of my early life: Don't stand out. What would I say? What was the point? I took lined paper along on a winter visit to San Francisco and began writing in longhand in an inspirational setting, overlooking the bay. The focal point that emerged was my tireless pursuit of a career in journalism.

It would be four years before I found Tom Driscoll and David Patt. With a writer's finesse, historical insight and poetic sensibility, David helped me flesh out my story via email through a long COVID winter, daily making it better. He is the best editor I've had in my long writing career. But there would be no David without Tom. He gave me a chance. I knew I was in good hands given the quality of the books he has published through his independent Shipwreckt press. When David and I let go of the manuscript, Tom and his wife Beth took over, applying well-honed wordsmithing and design skills to the finished product.

Where would I be without my Norwegian family? My brothers Verdon (spouse Renee) and Wayne (spouse Valerie) Hasleiet, sister Nancy (spouse Gary) Rustad, and our late parents Evelyn and Alfred Hasleiet; and Jon's parents, Ellen and Ted Halvorsen, added enormously to our lives.

Thanks to Doug Warren, my guardian angel, who was in contact almost daily after Jon died, and to other friends—Beth Murphy, Rik O'Neal and Joanne Lannin—who also kept in touch when I was in the throes of writing and grieving at the same time, as was Cordelia Onu, our caring Nigerian daughter, who has seen so much pain and loss of her own.

Thanks to my early, early readers long before Tom Driscoll and David Patt put their imprint on the book: Anne Kaplan, Doug Warren, Rik O'Neal and Barb Solberg.

I owe so much to the Journalism School at the University of Minnesota, whose staff and professors eased my difficult quest. So did three couples who became lifelong friends: Ellen and Roger Herdman, Anne and George Hage and Kathy and Skip Leabo.

And most of all, thank you to Roy Johnson, who started me on this journey.

Photo Credits

All photos submitted by the author with these exceptions:

James Lawson – Prince Lobel, Fair Use.
https://princelobel.com/professional/james-w-lawson/

Jeff Anderson – Anderson & Associates, Fair Use,
www.andersonadvocates.com/overview/attorney-profiles/

Kofi Annan – Fair Use, UN Photo/Mark Garten Kofi Annan